1885

INSTRUMENTAL ENGLISH

ON LINE

English for Computer Science

AF867879

Roberta Z. Lavine

Sharon A. Fechter

McGRAW-HILL

MADRID • BOGOTA • BUENOS AIRES • CARACAS
GUATEMALA • LISBON • MEXICO • NEW YORK
PANAMA • SAN JUAN • SÃO PAULO
AUCKLAND • HAMBURG • LONDON • MILAN
MONTREAL • NEW DELHI • PARIS • SAN FRANCISCO
SINGAPORE • ST. LOUIS • SIDNEY • TOKYO
TORONTO

Editorial Development:

Senior Project Editor:	Laurie Likoff
Design:	Catherine Gallagher
Photo Research:	Alice Lundoff
Cover Design:	Catherine Gallagher
	IBM

INSTRUMENTAL ENGLISH: ON LINE
English for Computer Science

ISBN 968-422-524-5

ISBN 0-07-036681-0

ISBN: 84-7615-794-0
Depósito legal: M. 39.508/1991
Impreso en Fernández Ciudad, S. L.
PRINTED IN SPAIN - IMPRESO EN ESPAÑA

TABLE OF CONTENTS

PREFACE

In recent years the interest in computer science and computer-related fields has increased dramatically. This text was written in order to provide the non-native speaker of English with an introduction to the field of computer science. The text is intended to promote success by familiarizing the student with the content, language structures, and vocabulary necessary for further study in the field.

The book is organized so that the types of language problems encountered by high intermediate or advanced English language students are incorporated within an appropriate context. These types of problems include the analysis and mastery of organizational patterns such as general to specific, or comparison and contrast, or grammatical structures such as modals and general tense usage. It is not intended that this be the student's first exposure to these organizational or grammatical points. Rather, the text is designed to provide practice, reinforcement, and further contextual application of these areas.

While the organizational and grammatical points are consistently presented, the specific technique or point chosen reflects the content of the individual chapter; that is, the points naturally reflect the logic of the content area. For example, *Chapter 3,* which treats the applications of computers in society today, lends itself to a progression from a general thesis statement to the presentation of specific and supporting details. Similarly, *Chapter 5,* which deals with the historical development of computers, uses a sequential organizational technique.

ORGANIZATION OF THE TEXT

The division of units is intended to allow the student to follow a natural learning curve from general, introductory considerations to specific, technical information. The first unit, "Computer Technology in Today's World," presents general considerations relevant to the importance of such technology to individuals and society. It contains basic computer literacy as well as areas of interest including careers, applications of computer technology, and current controversial issues. The second unit, "How We Got Where We Are," imparts an historical perspective. The evolution of computer technology, from the first to the fifth generation, is described in an effort to relate the past to the present with an eye to the future. Unit three, "Hardware: Micros to Mainframes," begins the presentation of technical content and vocabulary within a context and learning mode familiar to the English language learner. Concepts regarding computer hardware are presented, with special focus upon the microcomputer or the personal computer. The fourth unit, "Software: Theory to Application," presents detailed explanations of computer codes and introduces the students to computer languages and how they work. The basis for planning programs is presented in the chapter on flowcharts and emphasizes, in particular, the kind of logical thinking that might be required of the English language learner in further university studies. Such a configuration of units is designed to gradually ease the learner into the material without watering down or sacrificing the technical content, since that has proven to be the basis of student success in subsequent computer courses. This configuration also allows the text to be used in a variety of classroom situations: as the core text in an ESP course for computer science at the college or university level; as the primary text in a reading course for English language students who wish to become familiar with technical material; or, by emphasizing the first two units, as a general reader or computer literacy text for the ESL/EFL learner.

ORGANIZATION OF A LESSON

In terms of specific content, the text follows the general paradigm of an introductory course in data processing at the university level. The major content areas have been adapted for the English language learner at the *high-intermediate* or *advanced* level. Accordingly, the chapters present one or more major **structure points** that are inherent to the content. The focal point of each chapter is the **reading passage.** The reading is followed by vocabulary and comprehension exercises. **Vocabulary** is presented and practiced entirely in context. For this reason, vocabulary lists of definitions are not included in the individual chapters. Such a presentation would, naturally, defeat the purpose of vocabulary acquisition through context. Some of the vocabulary items, particularly those of a technical nature, may repeat from chapter to chapter for one or more of the following reasons: the word is used in a slightly different context, it is used in relation to a specific device, or it is repeated as a method of reinforcement. **Word study** and/or **language skill exercises,** which specifically relate to reading comprehension, follow. In the chapter on flowcharting, a technical skill inherent to the material and exclusive to the field of computer science is included. **Reading comprehension exercises** deal with specific details as well as general concepts. In addition, **enrichment activities** designed to enhance the cognitive as well as communicative capabilities of the language learner have been included.

RATIONALE

All of the exercises have been designed to follow a natural learning progression from recognition to production. In either a classroom or a self-study situation, the teacher or learner may want to review the word study and skill presentations prior to reading the passage. The exercises, however, are intended to be completed after the selection has been read, as they are an outgrowth of the content. The illustrations have been specifically chosen to aid in the comprehension of difficult concepts for both teachers and students.

Finally, this text is the result of more than three years germination and classroom contact with the type of language learner described above. We would, therefore, like to express our gratitude to all the students who have used these materials and whose comments and feedback have greatly contributed to their development.

It is hoped that this text will bridge the gap between the ESL/EFL classroom and that of the university or workplace. We have had great success with the materials contained herein. We wish you the same.

ACKNOWLEDGMENTS

1-1 General Electric Co.

1-2 Apple Macintosh C-28

1-3 Texas Instruments Corp.

2-1 AT&T

2-2 AT&T

2-3 AT&T

3-1 National Center for Atmospheric Research/National Science Foundation

3-2 IBM

3-3 Apple; IBM

3-4 IBM

4-0 RCA Picture Library

4-1 General Electric Co.

4-2 Hewlett Packard

4-3 IBM

5-2, 5-3 New York Public Library Picture Collection

5-4 AP/Wide World Photos

6-0 Texas Instruments Corp.

6-1, 6-2 IBM

6-3 Texas Instruments Corp.

6-4 IBM

7-1 IBM

7-2 Webster–McGraw-Hill

7-3 Apple Computer Corp.

7-4 IBM

7-5 Apple Computer Corp.

7-6 Apple Computer Corp.

7-7 AT&T

8-0 AT&T

8-3 McGraw-Hill Inc.

8-4 AT&T

8-5 RCA Picture Library

8-6 Apple Computer Corp.

9-1 AT&T

9-2 Apple Computer Corp.

9-3 IBM

9-4 IBM

10-0 Apple Computer Corp.

11-1 AT&T

11-3 Apple Computer Corp.

11-4 Apple Computer Corp.

11-5 IBM

12-0 UPI Photo/Michael Pugh

CHAPTER

1

INTRODUCTION TO COMPUTERS AND ELECTRONIC DATA PROCESSING

COMPUTERS AND SOCIETY

Computers have had a great effect on modern society and have caused a 1
great many changes in a short time. It is sometimes difficult to believe that computers first came into existence during the late 1930s, and that during this time, they were used mainly for scientific research in government and in universities. Computer technology has developed very quickly and has greatly influenced modern life. In fact, by the 1970s computers were used for applications that were previously unthinkable. By the 1970s, computers were common not only in businesses, which found them very helpful for all kinds of office tasks, but also in many other places, including retail stores, supermarkets, schools, and libraries. By the beginning of the 1980s computers could be found everywhere—in gas stations, in cars, or in household appliances such as dishwashers or microwave ovens, just to name a few examples (see illustration 1.1). In fact, by this time, microcomputers, or personal computers, relatively small and inexpensive computers (see illustration 1.2), were becoming even more common in both business and the home. Since the interest in computers is increasing every day, and because tremendous advances are being made so quickly in computer technology, it is often difficult to envision the impact that computers will have in the future.

1-1 Computers are now commonly found in household appliances such as dishwashers or microwave ovens.

1-2 Microcomputers, or personal computers, are popular in both business and the home.

COMPUTER TERMINOLOGY

Computers have brought about many changes in language, both in the 2
United States and in other countries. With the invention and use of the computer, an entire new vocabulary has developed—words which describe the computer and its functions, or relate to computer technology in some way. Such words include "software," the term used to refer to computer "programs." Programs are the instructions that tell the computer what to do. Software is generally contrasted with "hardware," the actual physical parts of the computer system (see illustration 1.3). "Debug" is another term that came into existence with computers. It means to locate and remove all mistakes in a computer program. Other computer-related words are not really new, but take on a special meaning in terms of computers. For example, "up" and "down," used in reference to computers, do not signify spatial relationships. Instead the term "up" means that the computer is "up" and working, while the term "down" means the opposite, that the computer is not functioning and cannot be used. Another example of a word which takes a special meaning in reference to computers is the word "boot." When used to refer to computers, "boot" is not used to mean a kind of shoe. Rather, "boot" is generally used as a verb. "To boot" a computer means to start it up.

1-3 "Hardware" refers to the actual physical parts of the computer system.

Other influences in language brought about by computer technology involve words which have become almost exclusively associated with computers, although they retain their original meanings. One such word is "user." While user really signifies "one who uses something," today it very often refers to a person using a computer. Associated with the word "user" is the term "user friendly." This is currently a very popular expression meaning that the computer can be easily understood and operated by non-technical, "non-computer" people. 3

Finally, many terms associated with computers are *acronyms*. An acronym is a word formed by the first letter or letters of all or some of the parts of a particular expression. Acronyms are very often used instead of the complete expression. Many languages used to program computers are acronyms. For example, the computer language BASIC is the acronym for *B*eginner's *A*ll-purpose *S*ymbolic *I*nstruction *C*ode. Another example of an acronym is PC, which stands for *p*ersonal *c*omputer. 4

WHAT IS DATA PROCESSING?

In spite of the tremendous impact computers have made and will continue to make on society, many people do not really understand what a com- 5 puter is or how it works. In fact, most people may not know much about computers except that using them usually makes their lives easier.

In very simple terms, a computer, regardless of its size, appearance, or cost, is a machine that processes data—facts—electronically. (Data is the plural of datum; however, in common usage, the word data is often used in the singular.) Processing data with a computer is relatively new; however, the idea of processing data is not. In general, data processing (DP) can be defined as a series of three steps: 1) the collection or gathering of data; 2) the manipulation or handling of data, and 3) the distribution or sending out of data or information for a particular purpose. Electronic data processing (EDP), therefore, is the collection, manipulation, and distribution of facts by electronic means—by computer. EDP has become the major method of processing data in modern society. In fact, it is so common that the general term data processing and the specific idea of electronic data processing have become synonymous and are now used interchangeably. 6

THE DATA PROCESSING CYCLE: INPUT, PROCESSING, OUTPUT

The data processing cycle takes place in three steps. First, data are put into a computer in a form the computer can understand. Second, the data are processed according to the instructions the computer receives through programs. Third, the data, now in a form understandable and meaningful to people, come out (see illustration 1.4). 7

DATA VERSUS INFORMATION

We have already mentioned that the facts which are put into the computer are called data. Data are raw facts or figures which are arranged in such a way that the computer can accept and process them. When data are put into, or "input" into, the computer, they may not be meaningful by themselves. Once the data have been handled or processed by the computer, they are changed into useful information. This useful information then comes out from, or is "output" by, the computer so that people can use it. This is the purpose of the computer, and of data processing—to process data so that they become useful information. 8

THE FORM OF DATA

In order for data to be processed by a computer, they must be "machine-readable," that is, expressed in a form the computer understands. Computers cannot deal with emotions, opinions, or feelings. All computer 9

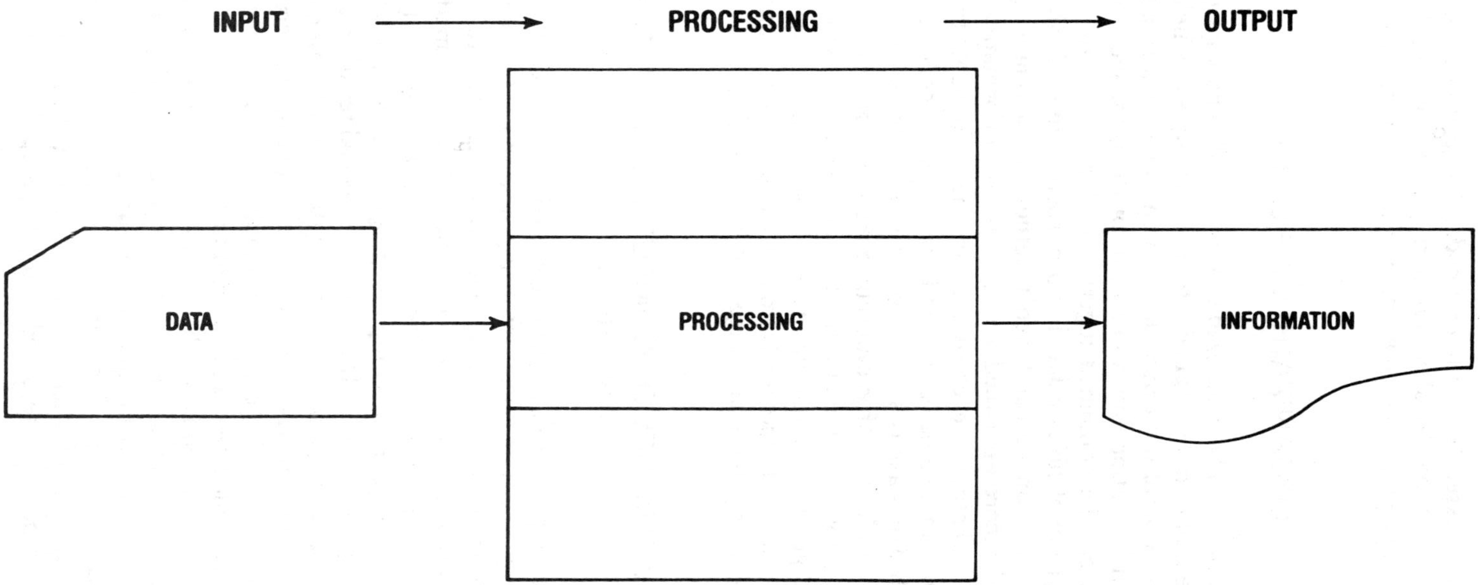

1-4 The data processing cycle takes place in three distinct steps.

information is expressed by a numeric code. The computer transforms everything—letters of the alphabet, numbers, punctuation marks, sounds, special symbols, etc.—into its own number system so that the data can be processed.

ORGANIZATION OF DATA

Data for a computer can be organized in several different ways (see illus- 10
tration 1.5). One unit of data is called a *field*. An example of a field may be a person's name. Several individual fields, such as a field for an individual's name, a field for nationality, and a field for the language a particular student speaks, can be combined together to form a *record*. A record, therefore, is a group of fields related to a particular unit of information. Records, like fields, can be combined together into a related group. A group of related records is called a *file*. A student information file may consist of individual records, each containing a name, nationality, and language field. Data can also be organized into very large collections called *data bases*. Each data base is a collection of related items which is organized so that it can be used for different purposes. For example, a data base containing information about an individual student's name, nationality, and language, like the one described above, could be used both to determine the number of students from a particular country and to classify students according to the language each individual speaks.

CHARACTERISTICS OF COMPUTERS: ACCURACY AND SPEED

Computers not only process data; they process data very accurately. Data 11
are processed by the computer by being transmitted electronically through the computer's circuits. Since electronic circuits rarely fail, the computer is almost always 100% correct. When a mistake is made it may not really be the computer's fault. The problem is usually due to human error, either to a mistake in the computer program or to a mistake in the data input into the computer. In fact, there is a special term, an acronym, to indicate that if badly organized or incorrect data are input into the computer, the information that is output will be meaningless. This term, GIGO, stands for *g*arbage *i*n, *g*arbage *o*ut and emphasizes the importance of using accurate data when dealing with computers.

Besides accuracy, speed is another characteristic of a computer. All 12
computer functions are carried out in very small units of time which are almost impossible for people to imagine. Two of these units are *microseconds* and *nanoseconds*. A microsecond is one-thousandth (1/1,000) of a second, while a nanosecond is one-billionth (1/1,000,000,000) of a second. The speed of a computer is measured in these units and is calculated by the time it takes to complete a particular job, such as adding numbers. A

DATA ORGANIZATION

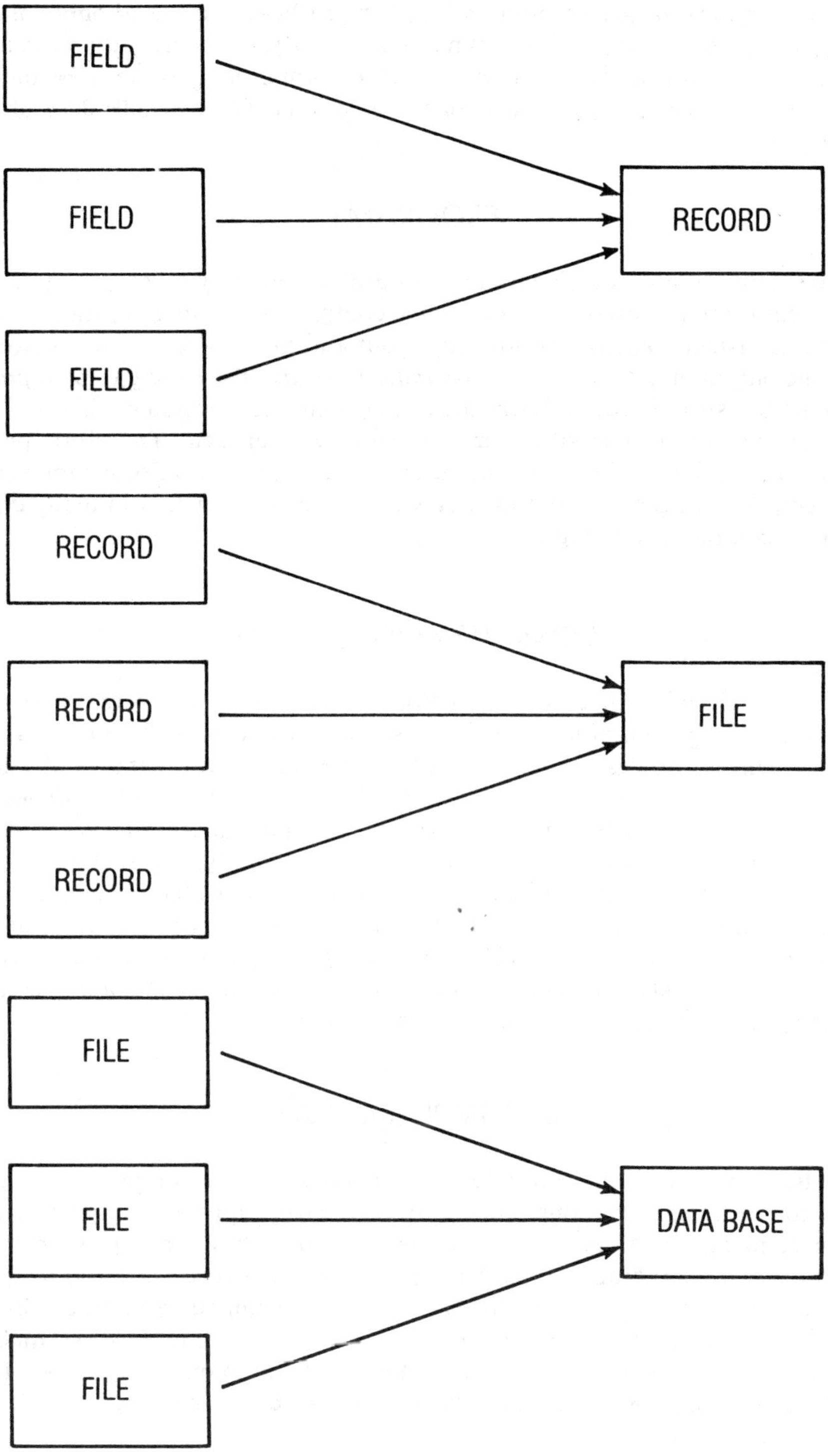

1-5

few smaller computers may need microseconds to complete a job while other, perhaps larger computers, work much faster and need only nanoseconds to do the same thing. While many computers currently measure speed in nanoseconds, in the near future computer speed may be measured in *picoseconds*, equal to one-trillionth (1/1,000,000,000,000) of a second.

PROGRAMS

While computers process data very accurately and very quickly, they can- 13
not think for themselves. In order for computers to function, they must receive instructions that control the input and processing of data, as well as the output of information. A *computer program*, also called a *stored program*, is a specific set of instructions that tells the computer what to do. Programs are not part of a computer; they are separate. Therefore, programs must be put into the computer, along with data, in order for processing to take place. Programs, or *software*, can be written in many different computer languages.

COMPUTER OPERATIONS

We have already stated that all types of computers, small personal com- 14
puters or large computers, work the same way and have the same basic cycle—input, processing, output. All computers are also capable of performing a small number of operations. These operations can be divided into three basic types: input and output operations (accepting facts and giving out information); arithmetic operations (adding, subtracting, multiplying, and dividing numbers); and logical operations (comparing numbers). These will be discussed further in connection with the computer system. With only these three types of operations, computers can accurately and quickly perform six major functions: storing, calculating, comparing, classifying, sorting, and summarizing.

THE COMPUTER SYSTEM

All the functions of the computer are carried out by the computer system. 15
All computer systems consist of three basic parts: input units, a processor unit, and output units (see illustration 1.6). *Input* units accept both the data and the programs needed for processing, and present them to the processor unit. *Output* units display the results obtained from processing. The *processor* unit, which both stores and processes data, has two main parts: the central processing unit (CPU), and the main storage unit. In addition, most computers also have some kind of auxiliary, or extra, storage.

1-6

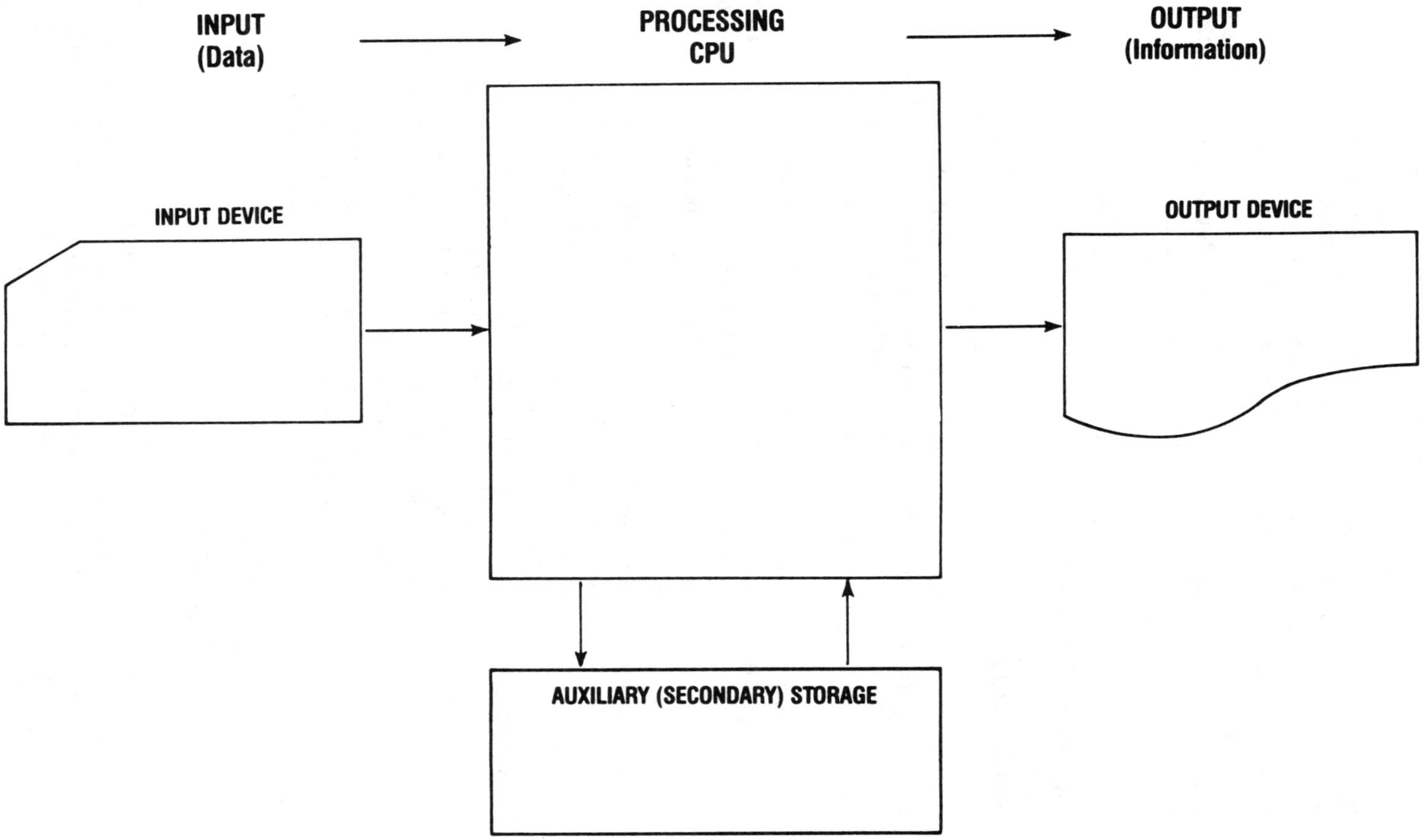

THE COMPUTER SYSTEM

SUMMARY

In summary, computers are devices that process data quickly and accu- 16
rately. Regardless of size, cost, or appearance all computers have the same basic cycle, are made up of the same basic parts, and perform the same types of operations. In spite of all their capabilities, however, computers need direction from people. Directed by human creativity and imagination, the use of computers will continue to develop, making these machines even more valuable in the future.

EXERCISES

Word Study

One of the most important skills for reading is that of understanding vocabulary from context. In order to understand new words from their context, you must look for clues that might tell you the meaning of the word. There are several different kinds of clues to look for.

1. Definitions/ Descriptions: Sometimes a definition or a description of the unknown word appears in the same sentence or a sentence near it. Look for words and phrases like "to mean," "to be," "to refer to," "to be called," "that is," etc.
2. Punctuation: Sometimes the meaning of the unknown word follows it in an appositive phrase or a parenthetical remark. Look for punctuation clues, especially commas, parentheses, and dashes.
3. Synonyms: Sometimes synonyms of the unknown word are given in the same sentence or another sentence. Look for pronouns which refer back to the word (this, that, these, those, it, they, them) and which might introduce the synonym.
4. Antonyms: Sometimes the meaning of an unknown word is understood from its opposite. Antonyms often appear in the same sentence as the unknown word or in a sentence near it.

Vocabulary from Context

A. Choose the letter of the word or expression that is closest in meaning to the first word or words. The number in parentheses indicates the paragraph in which the word can be found. Refer to the indicated paragraph as necessary. To help you, the kind of clue to look for is indicated.

1. hardware (2) (Look for a punctuation clue.)
   a. the physical parts of a computer
   b. the programs used with computers
   c. the fact that computers are hard to understand
2. debug (2) (Look for a definition in another sentence.)
   a. finding bugs in a computer
   b. finding and correcting errors in programs
   c. finding an insect and killing it
3. to boot (2) (Look for a definition in another sentence.)
   a. to find a shoe
   b. to put your foot in something
   c. to start up a computer
4. to input (8) (Look for a punctuation clue.)
   a. to put data into a computer
   b. to get data from a computer
   c. to put data into an objective form
5. machine-readable (9) (Look for a punctuation clue.)
   a. in a book read by a machine
   b. in a machine that reads books automatically
   c. in a form that machines can understand
6. data base (10) (Look for a definition in another sentence.)
   a. a base for a computer
   b. a file for data
   c. a large collection of data for various purposes
7. garbage in, garbage out (11) (Look for a definition.)
   a. if you take garbage in the house, someone else will take it out
   b. if bad data are put into a computer, bad data will come out
   c. if good data are put into a computer, bad data may come out

B. Match the word to the correct definition. Place the number of the word in column 1 that corresponds to the correct definition in column 2. Refer to the indicated paragraph as necessary.

1. file (10)	____	computer programs
2. nanosecond (12)	____	one-billionth of a second
3. data processing (6)	____	collecting, processing, and distributing data for a particular purpose
4. software (2)	____	a collection of records containing data

C. Fill in the blanks with one of the following words or terms from the reading. Refer to the indicated paragraph as necessary. Be sure to use the correct grammatical form.

appliance (1)	to envision (1)	function (2)
exclusively (3)	interchangeably (6)	manipulation (6)
operation (14)		

1. We use computers for applications that were difficult to imagine 30 or 40 years ago. The uses computers will have in the future are also hard ________________.
2. Electronic data processing and data processing are two terms which are really different; however, they have now become synonymous and are used ________________.
3. New words have been created to describe both computer technology and ________________.
4. Computers can be found in household ________________ such as ovens or dishwashers.
5. There are three basic types of computer ________________. input and output, mathematical calculations, and logical comparisons.
6. Data processing involves the handling or ________________ of facts and figures.
7. Some words associated with computers are not new, but are used almost ________________ in a computer-related context.

D. Find each of the following words or terms in the indicated paragraph in the reading. Then write a synonym, definition, or description of the word.

1. program (2)
2. up (2)
3. down (2)
4. field (10)

E. An acronym is a word formed by the initial letter or letters of all or some of the parts of an expression. Acronyms are generally written in capital letters.

Example: *B*eginner's *A*ll-purpose *S*ymbolic *I*nstruction *C*ode = BASIC

Write the acronyms for the following.

1. Data processing
2. Personal computer
3. Garbage in, garbage out
4. Central processing unit
5. Electronic data processing

Comprehension Exercises

A. True-False. Write a "T" if the statement is true. Write "F" if it is false.

1. Computer technology has changed little in the past 40 years.
2. It is difficult to imagine the impact computers will have on our lives in the future.
3. Computers have invented a new language.
4. All computer-related words are acronyms.
5. Many people do not really understand what computers are or how they work.
6. Electronic data processing is the most frequently used method of processing data.
7. Data and information are the same thing.
8. Computers can understand feelings.
9. Fields, records, and files are methods of organizing data.
10. Two characteristics of computers are speed and accuracy.
11. At the current time, computer speed is generally measured in picoseconds.
12. The basic cycle of all computers is output–processing–input.
13. There are two basic parts to all computer systems—input units and a processor unit.

B. Choose the letter of the *best* answer for each of the following.

1. Computer technology _____.
   a. was first developed in the 1960s
   b. has had a great impact on society over a long period of time
   c. first became popular in the 1970s
   d. has had a great impact on society over a short period of time
2. What is *not* true about computer technology and language?
   a. The acronym was invented by computers.
   b. New vocabulary words have come into existence.
   c. Some existing words have become almost exclusively associated with computers.
   d. Some words have taken on new meanings in a computer-related context.
3. User friendly means _____.
   a. the computer is a friend of the user
   b. the computer is easy to use and therefore "friendly" to the user
   c. the computer can be used only by friendly people
   d. the computer can be used only by people with technical skills

4. What is *not* a characteristic of EDP?
   a. Raw facts are input into the computer.
   b. Information is output by the computer in a form people can understand.
   c. Information is collected and transformed into raw facts.
   d. Data are collected, processed, and transformed into meaningful information.

5. Computer programs ____.
   a. are a permanent part of the computer
   b. are combined with data in order for processing to take place
   c. are written in English
   d. control input and output functions only

6. What is *not* a characteristic of all computers?
   a. speed
   b. accuracy
   c. large physical size
   d. input and output devices

Skill Enhancement

Reading for the Main Idea
Writing a Sentence that Expresses the Main Idea

In order to read with understanding, it is necessary to determine the central thought or the main idea of a passage. That is, in order to fully comprehend a text it is necessary to identify the topic of the passage and understand what the author is trying to say about it.

An entire reading selection, such as a chapter of a book or a long essay, has one main idea. The central idea of a long work is called the *theme*. Each paragraph of a long text will explain some aspect of the theme of the entire work.

In turn, each paragraph in a reading selection has a main idea. This is true of individual paragraphs which are not part of a longer work as well. The individual sentences in a paragraph support the main idea by describing, explaining, or detailing the central thought.

The main idea of a paragraph is sometimes stated or introduced by a sentence or several sentences. At other times, the main idea is not specifically expressed, but must be understood from the paragraph itself.

The main idea of a paragraph can be recognized by analyzing the following questions:

1. What idea is expressed by all or most of the sentences in the paragraph?
2. What idea do the sentences have in common?
3. What do the sentences in the paragraph describe?
4. About which subject does the paragraph provide details?
5. Structure used in the paragraph

A. Return to the beginning of this chapter and reread each of the indicated paragraphs. Then choose the statement which best expresses the main idea of the particular paragraph. A sample question has been done for you.

Paragraph 1

_____ a. Computers are found in many places.
_____ b. Computers have greatly changed our lives in a short time.
_____ c. It is difficult to predict the influence computers will have in the future.
_____ d. Computers have had some influence on modern life.

Explanation

_____ a. Computers are found in many places.

This is an example the author gives to show how computers have influenced society.

__X__ b. Computers have greatly changed our lives in a short time.

This is the main idea of the paragraph. All the examples focus upon the ways in which computers have influenced society and emphasize that the changes have come about in a short period of time.

_____ c. It is difficult to predict the influence computers will have in the future.

This is a conclusion the author draws based on the tremendous changes that have already taken place because of computers.

_____ d. Computers have had some influence on modern life.

This statement is not specific enough. The author stresses that computers have had a great effect on modern life and gives examples of the effects of computer technology.

1. Paragraph 2

_____ a. Some computer terms are new words.
_____ b. Computer terms describe the functions of the computer
_____ c. Some existing words have new meanings related to computers.
_____ d. Changes in language have resulted from the development of computer technology.

2. Paragraph 3

_____ a. Computer terminology is friendly.
_____ b. Computer-related terminology includes many acronyms and existing words used almost always in reference to computers.

_____ c. Computer vocabulary items include acronyms.
_____ d. Computer terms include popular expressions used almost exclusively in reference to computers.

3. Paragraph 6
_____ a. Computers process data.
_____ b. Data processing is the collection, handling, and distribution of data or information for a particular purpose.
_____ c. The idea of processing data has existed for a long time.
_____ d. Processing data with computers is somewhat new.

4. Paragraph 7
_____ a. Data processing involves three stages.
_____ b. Information is put into a computer.
_____ c. Information is output by a computer.
_____ d. Programs process the information in the computer.

B. Reread the indicated paragraphs and write a sentence which summarizes the main idea of the paragraph.

1. Paragraph 4
2. Paragraph 5
3. Paragraph 11

Recognizing and Writing a Topic Sentence

The main idea of a paragraph is sometimes stated, summarized, or introduced by one sentence in the paragraph. This sentence is called the *topic sentence.* The topic sentence is a very general statement and provides a focus for the paragraph. The topic sentence is often the first sentence in the paragraph; as such it generally states or introduces the main idea. If the topic sentence is the last sentence in the paragraph, it usually summarizes the central idea of the paragraph. The topic sentence may also occur in the middle of the paragraph. While it is common to write topic sentences for paragraphs, not every paragraph has a topic sentence or needs to have one.

A. Reread the indicated paragraphs. Then choose the sentence that is the most appropriate topic sentence for that paragraph. An example has been done for you.

Example: Paragraph 1—Computers have had a great impact on modern society and have brought about a great many changes in a relatively short time.

This is a topic sentence because it states the main idea of the paragraph—computers have influenced society and have brought about many changes in a short amount of time.

1. Paragraph 9
2. Paragraph 10
3. Paragraph 12
4. Paragraph 15

B. Write a topic sentence for the paragraphs indicated. They are paragraphs from the reading which have been modified.

1. Paragraph 8
   ______________________. Data are raw facts or figures which are arranged in such a way that the computer can accept and process them. When data are put into, or "input" into, the computer, they may or may not be meaningful. Once the data have been processed by the computer, the meaningless data are converted into useful information. This useful information then comes out from, or is "output" by, the computer so that people can use it. This is the purpose of the computer, and of data processing—to process data so that they become useful information.
2. Paragraph 13
   ______________________. A program is a specific set of instructions that tells the computer what to do. Programs are not part of a computer. Since they are separate, programs must be put into computers, along with the necessary data, in order for processing to take place. Programs can be written in many different computer languages.

Enrichment Activities

1. Give a short oral or written report summarizing what a computer is, how it works, and explaining what electronic data processing is. Be sure to use topic sentences in your report.
2. Find cartoons or short articles about computers in magazines or newspapers and interpret them using the information in this chapter.

CHAPTER 2

CAREERS IN DATA PROCESSING

Data processing, which is one of the most rapidly growing fields in the 1
world today, offers opportunities for many interesting careers. There are several types of jobs which are common to the field of data processing whether an individual works for a large corporation, a small business, a government agency, or a computer research and development company. The particular duties of each job may vary, however, depending upon a particular organization or company. In spite of the differences in individual jobs, there are several types of careers which are usually the same in any working environment. The types of jobs common in the data processing field may also be similar whether a person works with microcomputers or large mainframe computers. This chapter will examine some of the most typical careers found in the field of data processing (see illustration 2.1).

AREAS OF DATA PROCESSING: SYSTEMS ANALYSIS, PROGRAMMING, AND OPERATIONS

The data processing field is usually divided into three areas: systems anal- 2
ysis, programming, and operations. Systems analysis is the area which is concerned with the design and development of computer systems. Programming is the area which involves writing programs—instructions for the computer. These programs should implement the systems designed by the analysts. That is, they should get the systems working to accomplish the goals the analysts have specified. Finally, operations is the field of data processing that deals with the daily functions or operations of the computer system.

2-1 Data processing, one of the most rapidly growing fields in the business world, offers opportunities for many interesting careers.

THE DATA PROCESSING MANAGER

There are various computer professionals who carry out the different 3
functions of the data processing field. In many companies the three areas
which constitute all computer functions are supervised by a manager or
director of data processing. The data processing manager is responsible
for the administration of the entire computer department. Thus, he or she
not only directs and coordinates all the functions of the computer, but also
supervises all the personnel—the people—involved with computers. The
data processing director, who usually has many years of experience and
a college degree in computers or a related field, may often work directly
with the top management of the company where he or she is employed
(see illustration 2-2).

THE SYSTEMS ANALYST

Another job in the computer field is that of the systems analyst. The sys- 4
tems analyst often has a great deal of knowledge about computers and
computer operations. He or she is the data processing professional whose
job is to design and develop all the systems which will be used on a par-
ticular computer system. The systems analyst must first analyze the infor-
mation needs of his or her employer. He or she must then interpret the
company's needs and decide how to utilize the computer to fulfill them in
the most efficient way. In addition, the systems analyst must also know
how to program. Furthermore, as the systems analyst usually determines
what kind of equipment is best for a particular job, he or she must be an
expert in hardware as well as software.

Sometimes the systems analyst specializes in a particular field. For 5
example, the engineering or scientific analyst may work with international
communication systems. The commercial applications analyst, in con-
trast, is a person who deals with all the different aspects of the business
area. Another specialization within systems analysis is that of operations
research. Operations research is not only a very rapidly growing field
today, but is one which is generally considered to be very interesting and
challenging. The systems analyst who specializes in operations research
must make mathematical models of the various problems which are pre-
sented to him or her. These models are then used to provide a quantitative
or statistical basis for the decisions the analyst makes.

Systems analysts are usually required to have a college degree and 6
experience in the data processing field. They generally also have training
in and a knowledge of programming. In fact, many systems analysts know
programming very well because they were once programmers themselves.
Indeed, it is not at all unusual to find that many systems analysts are pro-
grammers who have been promoted.

THE COMPUTER PROGRAMMER

The systems analyst studies and solves a particular problem. He or she 7
then designs the systems that are needed to carry out the solution. After the systems analyst finishes the job, a programmer is consulted. The programmer is responsible for actually writing the programs for the systems designed by the analyst. The programmer first prepares a *flowchart,** a type of chart which illustrates the logic of the program. Next the programmer, who often knows several computer languages, chooses a language, and writes the program. Then he or she tests and debugs the program, correcting any mistakes which it might contain. Finally documentation—detailed explanations of the programmer's work—is prepared.

Like systems analysts, many programmers specialize in one field. 8
Such specialized programmers are called applications programmers. The applications programmer usually specializes in either business or science. A programmer may also specialize in developing software for the operating system of a computer. The operating system is a collection of pro-

*Flowcharts will be discussed in detail in Chapter 12.

2-2 The data processing manager is responsible for the administration of the entire computer department.

grams which are used to direct all of the different activities the computer carries out. The programmer who specializes in this type of software is called a systems programmer.

There are different levels of experience and responsibility in the field 9
of programming. Senior programmers, who are generally in charge of projects and have a great deal of experience and expertise, design complex flowcharts for programs. Junior programmers often code, that is, write instructions in a programming language, from the flowcharts designed by the senior programmers. Junior programmers may also develop small parts of a large program in order to acquire programming experience. Besides senior and junior programmers, some companies have programmer trainees. These trainees must go through on-the-job training before being allowed to code programs.

The skills required for these types of programming jobs depend upon 10
the level of responsibility of each position. A senior programmer's job usually requires experience and a college degree. A junior programming position might only require a college or high school degree. However, all programmers, especially those who must deal with a wide variety of computer applications, should have one important quality—a logical way of thinking.

THE COMPUTER OPERATOR

The area of computer operations deals with the daily activities of the com- 11
puter. Computer operators have many different responsibilities because they carry out the tasks that must be done regularly in order for the computer to function properly. For example, the operator starts up the computer system, and makes sure it is working correctly. The operator also organizes schedules and keeps records of all the work performed by the computer. Moreover, the computer operator often serves an apprenticeship in order to acquire the skills necessary to run the computer. During this training period, the operator may perform a variety of tasks including getting and setting up all necessary computer equipment.

OTHER JOBS IN DATA PROCESSING

Other jobs in the computer field include that of the data entry operator 12
and the program librarian. The data entry operator's job consists mainly of entering data into the computer. The program librarian is responsible for cataloging or keeping records of programs, data, etc. Still another very important position in data processing is that of computer technician. The technician, whose job is very important to the smooth operation of a computer system, fixes all the computer hardware.

JOBS WITH MICROCOMPUTERS

In large corporations the different positions in data processing may be sep- 13
arate jobs which are held by one individual. In other, perhaps smaller, companies, job responsibilities are often combined into one position such as programmer/analyst or programmer/operator. These types of combinations are especially common when dealing with microcomputers. While there are separate jobs for microcomputer analysts, programmers, or technicians, many companies combine all these jobs into one—the microcomputer specialist. Such a specialist is often expert in all aspects of personal computers. Another area which has grown in importance with the popularity of microcomputers is that of software evaluation or review. Many companies hire a person to look at all the software available for the type of personal computers they use. The software specialist then decides which programs will best meet the company's needs.

SUMMARY

Whether the duties and responsibilities of the data processing field are 14
divided into separate jobs or are combined into one position, the three areas of computing—systems analysis, programming, and computer operations—must be carried out by knowledgeable and experienced professionals in order for the computer to operate smoothly and successfully.

EXERCISES

Vocabulary from Context

A. Fill in the blanks with one of the following words or terms from the reading. Refer to the indicated paragraph as necessary. Be sure to use the correct grammatical form.

organization (1)	manager (3)	administration (3)	analyst (4)
challenging (5)	to promote (6)	to specialize (8)	to code (9)
to catalog (12)	to evaluate (13)		

1. The duties of the director of data processing are not the same in all companies. Some ____ or corporations may combine two or more jobs into one position.
2. A scientific programmer usually has a great deal of knowledge about his or her area. He or she ____ in scientific applications.
3. A data processing professional who examines and interprets the information needs of a company is a systems ____.

4. The data processing ____ is in charge of the entire computer department.
5. The junior programmer ____ or writes a program from a flowchart.
6. Many systems analysts were once programmers who were ____ to jobs of greater responsibility.
7. The program librarian keeps records of and ____ the programs a company has.
8. The data processing manager is responsible for the ____ of the entire computer department. He or she supervises all the functions of the computer department as well as the employees.
9. The area of operations research is very exciting. It is a ____ and rewarding field.
10. A software specialist reviews or ____ software to see if it meets the needs of a particular company or individual.

B. Find each of the following words or terms in the indicated paragraph in the reading. Then write a synonym, definition, or description of the word or term.

1. management (3)
2. personnel (3)
3. quantitative (5)
4. expertise (9)
5. apprenticeship (11)

Now use the correct word to complete the following sentences.

1. Operations research analysts develop mathematical models in order to provide ____ reasons for making decisions.
2. The systems analyst works with the top ____ of a company to determine the needs of the corporation.
3. People with no experience or training must serve an ____ to learn about computers and work in the field.
4. An experienced applications programmer in business has ____ in writing programs for companies.
5. Programmers, analysts, operators, and clerical and technical people are some of the ____ that make up the data processing department.

Comprehension Exercises

A. True-False. Write a "T" if the statement is true. Write "F" if it is false.

1. Data processing can be divided into three general areas.

2. The function of data processing which is concerned with the daily operations of the computer system is that of systems analysis.
3. The manager of data processing is the individual responsible for all areas of computer functions and all computer personnel.
4. The systems analyst is required to know about software only.
5. The systems analyst designs and develops computer systems.
6. Operations research involves investigation in the medical field.
7. Programmers write programs which carry out the systems designed by analysts.
8. Programmers who specialize in a particular area are called applications programmers.
9. The systems programmer specializes in software for the computer's operating system.
10. Programmers do not have to think logically.
11. One of the duties of the computer operator is to start up the computer system.

B. Choose the letter of the best answer for each of the following.

1. Which is a false statement about the data processing profession?
   a. Systems analysis refers to the design of the entire computer system.
   b. Programmers work with systems analysts.
   c. Operations refers to the daily operations of the computer.
   d. Systems analysis refers to the daily functions of the computer system.

2. What are the duties of the director of data processing?
   a. starting up the computer
   b. making money
   c. supervision of the computer system and data processing personnel
   d. analysis of the computer system and the design of programs

3. What are the responsibilities of a systems analyst?
   a. analyzing the information needs of a company and designing systems to meet these needs
   b. starting up the computer and programming
   c. programming and maintaining the program library
   d. working with international communications and microcomputers

4. What is *not* true about programmers and programming?
   a. Programmers write instructions for computers so that data can be processed correctly.
   b. Applications programmers specialize in one area.

c. Systems programmers write programs for scientific applications.
d. Programmers may have positions on the senior, junior, or trainee level.

5. The microcomputer specialist ____.
   a. knows nothing about microcomputers
   b. owns a microcomputer
   c. knows a great deal about microcomputers
   d. sells microcomputers

6. Which is *not* a job in the data processing field?
   a. manager of data processing
   b. applications programmer
   c. data entry operator
   d. telephone operator

Skill Enhancement

Restrictive and Nonrestrictive Adjective Clauses

An adjective clause is a subordinate clause which modifies the noun or pronoun which precedes it in the main clause. Adjective clauses generally occur immediately after the noun or pronoun they modify. This noun or pronoun is called an antecedent.

Relative pronouns are used in adjective clauses to introduce that clause. The relative pronouns *who* and *that* refer to people and replace the subject of the adjective clause. The relative pronouns that replace the subject when referring to things are *which* and *that.*

Example: A programmer is a person *who* writes computer programs. Programs are series of instructions *which* tell the computer what to do.

Relative pronouns also replace the object of the adjective clause. The pronoun *whom* is formally used to refer to people. In informal usage *who* and *that* are used. The pronoun *which* is used to refer to things. In addition, in object adjective clauses the relative pronoun is often omitted.

Example: The programmer writes programs for the analyst *(whom)* he knows well.

The relative pronouns *whom* (for people) and *which* (for things) are used after prepositions.

Example: The woman for *whom* I work is a senior programmer.

Other relative pronouns include *whose* (possessive), *where* (adverb of location) to replace a preposition + which, and *when* (adverb of time) to replace a preposition + which.

Example: The technician *whose* job is to fix the computer has been working for a long time.
The department in *which* (where) I work is systems operations.

There are two kinds of adjective clauses—restrictive and nonrestrictive.

Restrictive clauses single out the antecedent and limit or define the group that the person or thing belongs to. A restrictive clause adds information to the sentence and tells *which* or *what kind.* A restrictive clause cannot be omitted without changing the basic meaning of the sentence. Restrictive clauses are never set off by commas.

Example: The applications programmer is the data processing professional *who writes programs which have a specific purpose or application.*

Nonrestrictive clauses do not add basic information to the sentence. They do not limit or define the antecedent of the main clause in any way.

Because they do not tell *which* or *what kind,* the nonrestrictive adjective clause may be omitted from the sentence without changing the original meaning. Nonrestrictive adjective clauses are set off by commas.

Example: The data processing manager, *who supervises the computer department,* has a lot of experience working with people and computers.

A. Read the following paragraph and fill in the blanks with an appropriate relative pronoun. The paragraph has been modified from one in the text.

The systems analyst is the professional ____________ studies and solves a particular problem. He or she then designs the systems ____________ are needed to carry out the solutions he or she has devised. After the systems analyst finishes the job, a programmer is consulted. It is the programmer ____________ is responsible for actually writing the programs ____________ allow the computer to carry out the processing as designed by the analyst. The programmer, ____________ job is to code the program, generally prepares a flowchart ____________ illustrates the logic of the program. Next the programmer, ________ often knows several computer languages, chooses a language and codes the program. Then the programmer tests and debugs the program, correcting any mistakes ____________ the program might contain. Finally he or she prepares the documentation, detailed explanations ____________ clarify all aspects and procedures of the programmer's work.

B. Decide whether the following sentences contain restrictive or nonrestrictive adjective clauses. Put commas around the nonrestrictive clauses.

1. Data processing a field which is one of the most rapidly growing in the world today offers opportunities for many interesting careers.
2. Systems analysis is the area which is concerned with the overall design and development of the computer system.
3. In many companies the three areas which constitute all computer functions are supervised by a manager or director of data processing.
4. The systems analyst who specializes in operations research must formulate mathematical models of the various problems which are presented by management.
5. The systems analyst who spends a great deal of time working with the management of a company must know how to program.

C. Rewrite the following sentences, including the second sentence in the first as an adjective clause. Substitute a relative pronoun for the underlined words. Remember to use commas to set off nonrestrictive clauses; do not use commas with restrictive clauses.

Example: Programmers are very qualified professionals. These programmers can write both systems and applications programs.
Programmers who can write both systems and applications programs are very qualified professionals.

Example: Systems analysts are experts in hardware and software. They design and develop computer systems.
Systems analysts, who design and develop computer systems, are experts in hardware and software.

1. The data processing manager supervises the data processing department. The data processing manager deals with top management.
2. Programmers write programs to carry out the systems designed by analysts. The analysts determine the information needs of the company.
3. The computer operator may serve an apprenticeship. This apprenticeship helps him or her to acquire the skills needed to run the computer.
4. The programmer codes programs in a programming language. The job of the programmer is to first prepare a flowchart.
5. A company presents problems to an operations research analyst to solve. The problems will be represented by mathematical models.
6. Operators and programmers report to the manager of data processing at the company. They are employed at the company.
7. Programmers develop programs for the systems designed by analysts. The programmers consult with the analysts.
8. Programmers develop programs for the systems designed by analysts. The programmers consult with the analysts.
9. An important part of data processing is operations. Operations deals with the daily functions of the computer.

Word Transformations

Words have many different but related forms. The meanings of words in the same family may be similar, but take on a special significance according to their function in the paragraph.

Some word families are composed of a verb representing a specific action, a noun which represents the performance of the action, another noun, formed with the suffix *-er* or *-or* representing a person who performs the action, and an adjective relating to the verb.

Example:

verb (action)	**noun (performance)**	**noun (performer)**	**adjective (relating to)**
administer	administration	administrator	administrative
manage	management	manager	manageable
program	programming	programmer	programmable
operate	operations	operator	operational

A. Study the following word transformations. Then complete the paragraphs with the correct form of the indicated word according to its meaning. Some forms of the word can be found in the reading passage, but others cannot.

1. administer
The data processing ____ has a difficult job. He or she is in charge of the entire ____ of the analysis and programming functions. He or she ____ all of the daily computer operations as well. Sometimes the ____ duties of the manager of data processing seem never-ending.

2. manage
The person who ____ the data processing department is called the ____ of data processing. He or she takes care of the ____ of all the department's employees and equipment. If this person is not very organized, his or her job will not be very ____.

3. program
A ____ is a very important person in the data processing department. He or she ____ for a variety of applications. Sometimes the ____ the ____ writes may be simple. Other times, if a task is not well suited to the computer, it may not really be ____. In this case, the ____ job can be very difficult.

4. operate
One of the areas of data processing is the daily ____ of the computer. The computer ____, who ____ the computer, must make sure that the computer is running correctly. If the computer is not ____, the ____ must find the problem and correct it.

Some word families are composed of a verb representing a specific action, a noun which is the result of that particular action, and another noun, formed with the suffix *-ist, -er* or *-or,* representing a person who performs the action.

Example:

verb (action)	noun (result of action)	noun (performer of action)
analyze	analysis	analyst
develop	development	developer
specialize	specialization	specialist

B. Fill in the blanks with the appropriate form of the word.

1. analyze
   One important area of data processing is systems ____. The systems ____ must examine all aspects of a company's problem. He or she must ____ hardware and software requirements, the specific instructions the company provides, and many other things.
2. specialize
   The applications programmer ____ in one area. If the programmer is a ____ in business, his or her programming ____ is writing programs in a language designed for business applications.
3. develop
   The ____ of a system is a difficult task. The ____ must ____ a system to meet the needs of a particular company.

Enrichment Activities

1. Give an oral or written report describing several of the data processing careers discussed in this chapter, or about other jobs in the data processing field. Be sure to use adjective clauses in your description.

2. Interview someone working in the computer field. Gather information about his or her job and the specific duties of the position. Using adjective clauses, describe this person and his or her work.

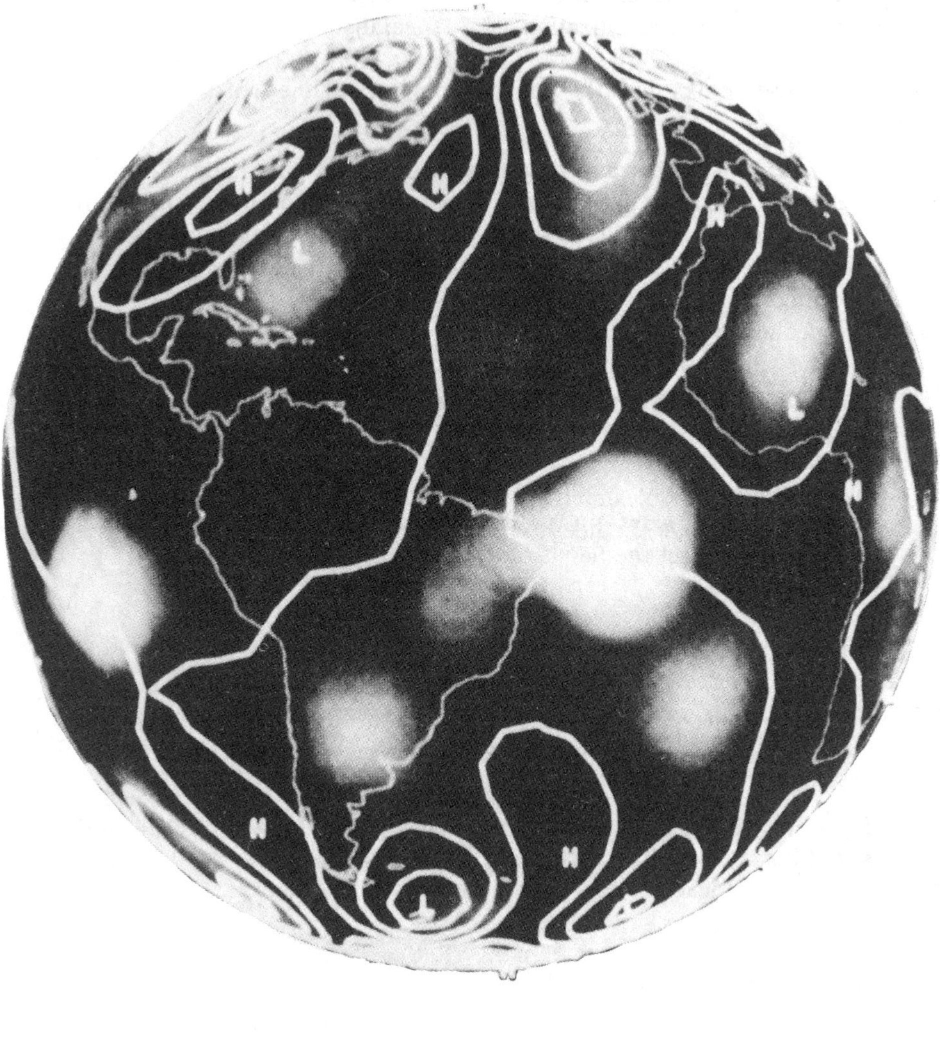

CHAPTER 3

CURRENT APPLICATIONS OF COMPUTER TECHNOLOGY

Computer technology affects every aspect of modern life. There are thousands of areas currently influenced by such technology and new applications are being developed daily. Computers have numerous uses and applications. Among the areas that currently use computer technology a great deal are business and industry, government, and medicine. Scientists, educators, and artists also employ the computer to assist them in their work and to enable them to use their time more creatively. In addition, computer technology has had a significant effect on entertainment and the arts. Computers have even begun to affect the home lives of their users. 1

COMPUTERS IN BUSINESS

Perhaps the greatest effect of computer technology on modern society may be seen in the business field. The vast majority of businesses commonly use electronic data processing (see illustration 2.1). Computers are employed in this field not only for everyday tasks, such as payroll, inventory, and billing, but they are also used for more complex operations, such as budgeting, research and development, and planning. Computers perform these functions for practically all types of businesses. In response to the specific demands of individual businesses, however, various special- 2

3-1 The government's official weather forecasts are dependent upon computer-produced data, such as weather maps and satellite communications.

ized hardware and software systems have been developed. Large businesses, such as a telephone company, might utilize a large, powerful mainframe computer, whereas small businesses, such as gift shops, might employ a personal business computer. Many businesses make use of computers, particularly personal computers, to help with secretarial tasks. Word processing programs help secretaries complete typing tasks more quickly and efficiently. The same computer that is used for word processing may also be used to help with the accounting tasks of both large and small businesses. Many businesses might combine the use of a large, powerful computer with that of small, personal computers.

Banks, for example, rely almost entirely upon electronic data pro- 3
cessing to perform their complex operations of check clearing and collection. Large retail stores and chains, such as supermarkets and department stores, make extensive use of computers not only to maintain strict inventory control, but also to record sales. Airlines, railways, and hotels depend upon computer systems to make reservations for their clients. Other aspects of travel, including loading cargo, scheduling flights and trains, and operating instruments, are also computer controlled. The printing and publishing industries also depend on computers, since modern printing methods are computerized.

Computerized control systems have many different applications. Such 4
control systems are essential to the efficient operation of many businesses. Automobile factories, for example, employ a computerized system to control the operation of production lines. An increasing number of manufacturing organizations are now using computer-controlled robots on their assembly lines. In food plants, clothing factories, and pharmaceutical companies, computerized control systems perform the functions of filling containers, cutting patterns, and sealing bottles.

COMPUTERS IN GOVERNMENT

Although businesses use computers a great deal, federal, state, and local 5
governments constitute the largest group user of computers in the United States. Record-keeping functions, necessary for such tasks as processing payroll, deducting taxes, and maintaining social security data, make up one of the government's primary uses of computers. In fact, the U.S. Bureau of the Census led the early development and use of computer technology.

The Bureau of the Census is not the only large government agency 6
which relies heavily upon computer technology. The work performed by government agencies like the Internal Revenue Service (IRS), the Federal Bureau of Investigation (FBI), the National Security Agency (NSA), the National Aeronautics and Space Administration (NASA), and the Environmental Protection Agency (EPA) would be impossible without the aid of computers.

Computer technology is especially important to ensure the smooth 7
operation of the Department of Defense (DOD). Computers coordinate the systems of various branches of the armed services—the Army, the Navy, the Air Force, and the Marines. In fact, computer technology has become absolutely necessary to the armed forces. Computers are essential in the development of military weapons and complex defense systems. In addition, computer simulations of real situations have proven to be very helpful in training military personnel. Although a soldier once relied primarily upon the excellence of his vision to sight and hit a target, he now depends almost entirely upon the accuracy of the computer to complete this task.

Law enforcement agencies on the federal level, particularly the FBI, 8
require advanced computer technology to perform such sophisticated tasks as matching fingerprints and identifying voice patterns. State and local law enforcement agencies utilize the computer in accomplishing a variety of tasks, including monitoring weapons sales, collecting fines, issuing license plates, and even registering puppy dogs. Computers are essential not only in fighting crime, but also in preventing it. Computer-based analyses can indicate the areas of high crime incidence, as well as predict future patterns of criminal activity.

Computers play a part in almost every area of government. The gov- 9
ernment's official weather forecasts are dependent not only upon computer-produced data, including weather maps (see illustration 3.1), but also upon computer-controlled communications for satellites. City-operated subway systems, like the one in Washington D.C., are often directed by computers as well. Even traffic signals are operated by means of computerized control systems like those utilized in business and industry.

COMPUTERS IN SCIENCE

Besides their importance in business and government, computers are also 10
very important in scientific fields. Geologists, for example, use computer technology to discover new deposits of energy resources; oceanographers use computers to obtain and process data concerning marine life, and botanists use computer-controlled instruments to analyze the composition of plants. Space exploration would be impossible without computers. Not only do computers control the operation of spacecraft, but they also provide the data astronauts need to make their calculations. As old as the science of astronomy is, advances such as the telescope at Mt. Palomar would have been unthinkable without computer technology.

COMPUTERS IN MEDICINE

Computers are used in the field of health care for various purposes. Main- 11
taining accounts and other administrative duties are performed by the

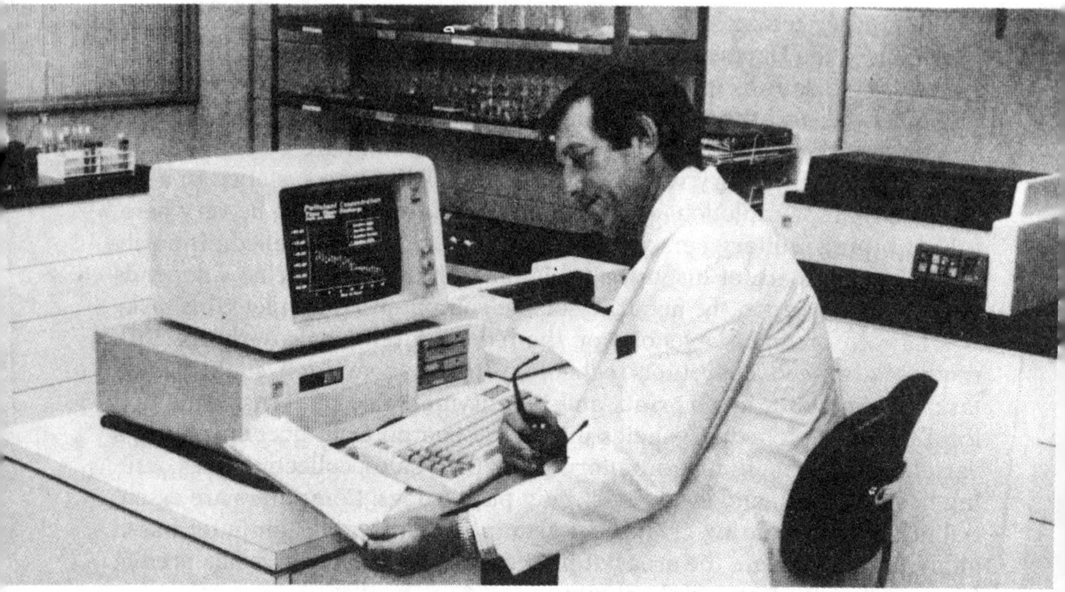

3-2 In medicine, patient care functions are often computer controlled.

3-3 In education, computers are utilized to keep student records and further educational research, as well as assist in educating the student.

computer. In addition, patient care functions are often computer controlled. Computers monitor, or watch, a patient's vital signs, such as heart rate, blood pressure, and temperature. This allows for better quality health care because doctors and nurses have the opportunity to devote more time to individual patients. Up-to-date medical information and personal patient histories can be obtained immediately. Therefore, computers also aid medical personnel by helping them make intelligent decisions in life-threatening situations. In fact, the Centers for Disease Control in Atlanta, Georgia, provide and receive essential medical data on both a national and international scale. Such life-saving information is then analyzed and stored in a large data base so that it may be readily available when it is needed (see illustration 3.2).

COMPUTERS IN EDUCATION

In education, computers are utilized not only to keep student records and further educational research, but also to assist in educating the student. Computer-assisted instruction (CAI) refers to the direct communication between a student and a computer. The purpose of this communication is either to teach or practice specific educational material. The use of computers in education is very promising because the computer can serve a large number of students individually. CAI now influences educational practices on all levels of instruction (see illustration 3.3). 12

COMPUTERS IN THE ARTS AND ENTERTAINMENT

Just as computers have proven to be beneficial in such fields as business, government, science, and education they have become equally important to the arts and entertainment. There can be no doubt that computers can be effectively employed for creative purposes. They are used by graphic artists, sculptors, and writers. Computers are an important tool in modern animation (cartoons) and can even be employed to compose music. Computers have also had a significant effect upon the entertainment field, as can be seen by the great popularity of computerized games. The motion picture and television industries also demonstrate the varied uses of computers. The special effects so popular in contemporary movies would be impossible without computer technology. 13

COMPUTERS IN THE HOME

With the growing popularity of microcomputers, computer technology now affects home life as well. Many adults employ microcomputers to either supplement their children's education or to enrich their own knowl- 14 edge. Even pre-school children benefit from the use of home computers. The growing popularity of personal computers is shown by the increasing use of such small computers not only for education or home entertainment, but also for such household tasks as planning menus, projecting budgets, and balancing checkbooks. Indeed, the once far-fetched dream of a computer-controlled home is fast becoming a reality (see illustration 3.4).

SUMMARY

These are just a few of the many applications of computer technology 15
today. The number of applications of computer technology is increasing every day and the number of people using computers is increasing as well. It is very likely that within the next few years few areas will remain untouched by computer technology.

EXERCISES

Vocabulary from Context

A. Fill in the blanks with one of the following words or terms from the reading. Refer to the indicated paragraph as necessary. Be sure to use the correct grammatical form.

applications (1)	to enable (1)	vast (2)
marine (10)	increasing (14)	far-fetched (14)

1. Ideas, such as space exploration, that were once considered ____ are now a reality.
2. The ____ majority of large corporations employ general purpose computers.
3. The ____ popularity of microcomputers will ultimately result in a decrease in the cost of these devices.
4. By freeing us from routine tasks, computers ____ us to use our time more creatively.
5. Data concerning ____ life gathered during underwater expeditions are analyzed by computers.
6. One of the many ____ of computer technology in the business field is to control inventory.

B. Find each of the following words or terms in the indicated paragraph in the reading. Then write a synonym, definition, or description of the word or term. Use your dictionary only if necessary.

1. inventory (2)
2. billing (2)
3. geologist (10)
4. oceanographer (10)
5. botanist (10)

Now use the correct word to complete the following sentences.

1. A person who studies plant life is a ____.
2. A ____ studies the composition of the earth.
3. A specialist in marine science is an ____.
4. Businesses rely on a periodic ____ to keep track of their merchandise.
5. ____ is the primary method by which businesses collect revenues.

C. Write the acronyms for the following.

1. Department of Defense
2. Internal Revenue Service
3. National Aeronautics and Space Agency
4. Federal Bureau of Investigation
5. National Security Agency
6. Environmental Protection Agency
7. Computer-assisted Instruction

Comprehension Exercises

A. True-False. Write a "T" if the statement is true. Write "F" if it is false.

1. The use of computers by the government is limited to the Bureau of the Census.
2. Modern animation and special effects are largely dependent upon computer technology.
3. Business, government, science, and education make use of computer technology.
4. Assembly lines are all controlled by hand.
5. Computer technology has had no effect on the field of music.
6. The computer-controlled home is now common in the United States.
7. Children in the primary grades make use of the computer.
8. NASA uses computers to match fingerprints.
9. The greatest effect of computer technology can probably be seen in the business field.
10. Computers help people use their time creatively.

B. Choose the letter of the *best* answer for each of the following.

1. Which of the following is *not* mentioned in the reading as an application of computer technology?
   a. traffic control
   b. payroll
   c. car maintenance
   d. animation

2. Computer-controlled robots are used in ____.
   a. education
   b. manufacturing
   c. hotels
   d. menu planning

3. CAI is employed ____.
   a. only in high schools in large cities
   b. only in colleges and universities
   c. only on microcomputers
   d. on all levels of instruction

4. The Department of Defense utilizes computers ____.
   a. only to sight targets
   b. only to design weapons
   c. to ensure the smooth operation of all military activity
   d. primarily to reduce crime

5. Which of the following is *not* a computer application in the field of health care?
   a. administering drugs
   b. monitoring vital signs
   c. researching diseases
   d. maintaining patient records

3-4 Even pre-school children benefit from the use of home computers.

Skill Enhancement

Parallelism

Parallelism involves the use of similar grammatical structures, either in a series or between dependent or independent clauses.

A. Parallelism in a series

Example: Record-keeping functions necessary for such tasks as processing payroll, deducting taxes, and maintaining social security data make up one of the government's primary uses of computers.

The series "processing payroll, deducting taxes, and maintaining social security data" constitutes the use of parallelism in this sentence. The parallel structures are composed of a series of gerund phrases.

B. Parallelism between clauses

Example: Although a soldier once relied primarily upon the excellence of his vision to sight and hit a target, he now depends almost entirely upon the accuracy of the computer to complete this task.

The sequence of parallel structures between these clauses is: Subject + Verb phrase + Prepositional phrase + Infinitive Phrase

C. Faulty Parallelism

The incorrect use of parallelism, or faulty parallelism, involves the use of dissimilar grammatical structures within a series or between clauses.

Example: Record-keeping functions, necessary for such tasks as processing payroll, deducting taxes, and to maintain social security data, comprise one of the government's primary uses of computers.

This sentence illustrates faulty parallelism in the use of the infinitive phrase: (gerund phrase + gerund phrase + infinitive phrase).

Example: Although a soldier once relied primarily upon his excellent vision to sight and hit a target, he now depends almost entirely upon the accuracy of the computer to complete this task.

By substituting "his excellent vision" for the "excellence of his vision," the parallelism between the clauses is disrupted.

A. Decide whether the parallelism in the following sentences is correct or faulty. If the sentence exhibits faulty parallelism, identify the incorrect element or elements. These sentences are based on the reading.

1. State and local law enforcement agencies utilize the computer in accomplishing a variety of tasks, including monitoring weapons sales, collecting fines, issuing license plates, and even registering puppy dogs.
2. In food plants, clothing factories, and pharmaceutical companies computerized control systems perform the functions of filling containers, pattern cutting, and sealing bottles.
3. Other aspects of air and rail travel, including loading cargo, scheduling flights and trains, and operating instruments are computer controlled.
4. Computers are essential not only in fighting crime, but also in the prevention of it.
5. In education, computers are utilized not only to keep student records and further educational research, but also in assisting in educating the student.

B. Correct the faulty parallelism in the following sentences. These sentences are not found in the reading.

1. A computer programmer doesn't need an advanced degree, only having some training.
2. A good programmer knows how to define a problem, plan a program, and analyzes data as well.
3. Modern computers are faster, cheaper, and can be relied on much more than older computers.
4. The computer has several functions. Among them are sorting, summarizing, storing, and the classification of data.
5. Computers are used for keeping records, to maintain inventories, and to collect bills.

Skill Enhancement

Paragraph Organization—General to Specific

Many different organizational techniques are utilized in writing. In order for the reader to fully comprehend the reading material, he or she should understand these techniques. The organization of this reading is based upon the progression from the general to the specific. A broad concept is presented by way of introduction in the reading as a whole and within individual paragraphs. The particular details supporting the general concept are then given. It is important to pay particular attention to the topic sentence because this often indicates the progression from one area to another. For example, the sentence "Besides their importance in business and government, computers are also instrumental in all scientific fields" makes the transition between the topic just discussed and the one to follow. The topic sentence may also indicate that details are to follow: "Computers are used in the field of health care for a variety of purposes."

A. Identify the organizational components of this reading by filling in the following outline. Part of the outline is completed for you. Remember that a general concept, in this case areas that computer technology has affected, is supported by specific details.

Computer Technology in Modern Life
(General Concept)

I. Business
   A. Banking
   B. Retail
   C. Travel
   D. Printing and publishing
   E. Manufacturing

II. Government
   A. Record-keeping agencies
   B. ____________________
   C. Department of Defense
   D. ____________________
   E. ____________________
   F. ____________________

III. Science
   A. Geology
   B. ____________________
   C. ____________________
   D. ____________________
   E. ____________________

IV. ____________________
   A. ____________________
   B. Patient care functions
   C. ____________________

V. Education
   A. Student records
   B. ____________________
   C. ____________________

VI. The Arts and entertainment
   A. ____________________
      1. Graphic artists
      2. ____________________
      3. ____________________
      4. ____________________
      5. ____________________
   B. Entertainment
      1. ____________________
      2. ____________________
      3. Television

VII. ____________________
   A. ____________________
   B. ____________________
   C. Household management
      1. ____________________
      2. ____________________
      3. ____________________

Enrichment Activities

1. Write a composition using the organizational technique of general to specific on one of the following topics:

   A. The Effect of Computers in Your Profession
   B. The Effect of Computers in the Future

2. Prepare and present an oral or written report concerning the effect of computer technology on a particular business, government agency, scientific or educational institution, or entertainment enterprise in your area.

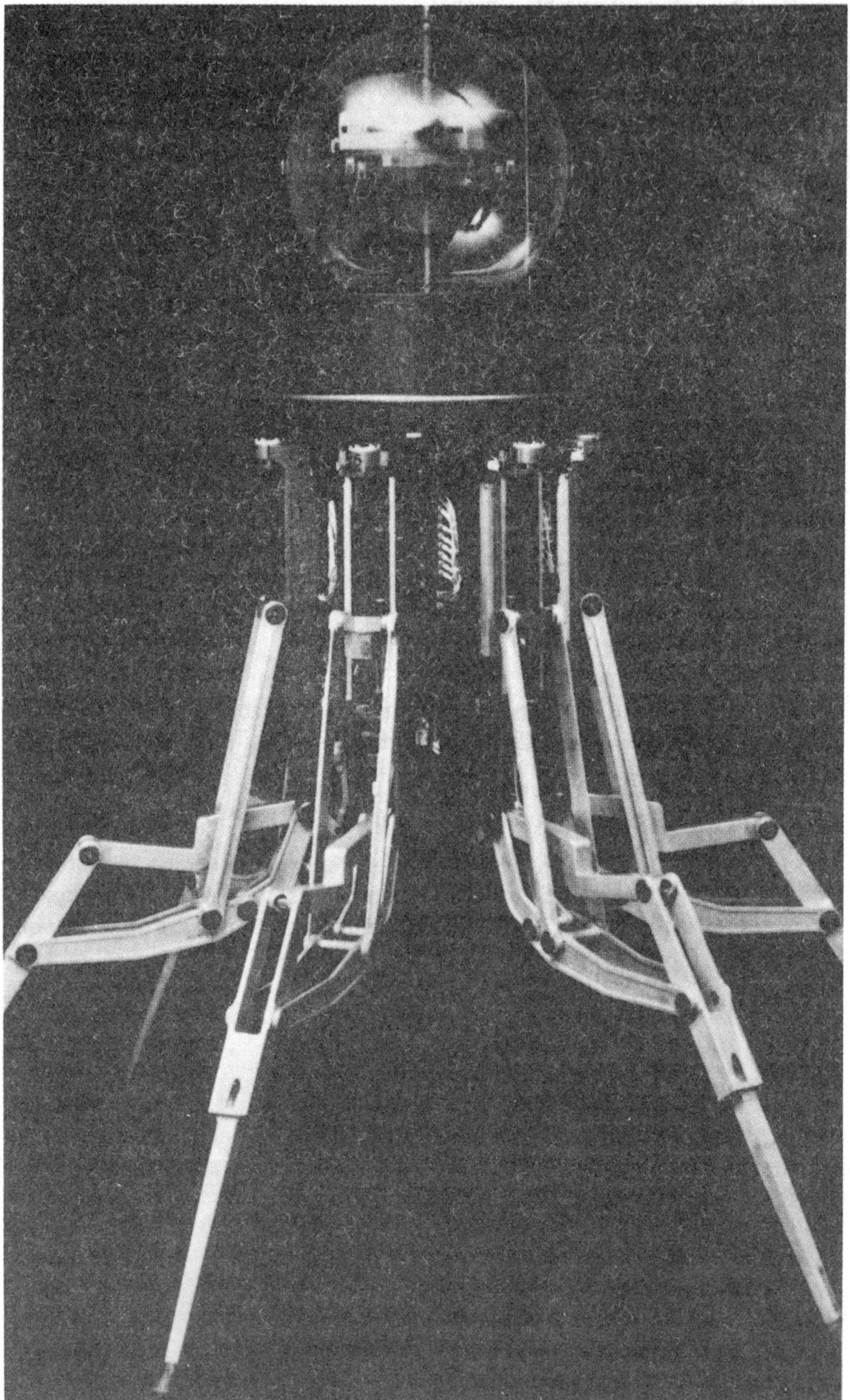

CHAPTER 4

CURRENT ISSUES IN DATA PROCESSING

Many problems have resulted from the prominent role computers play in 1
modern society. Among the issues and controversies associated with computers are the following: negative attitudes toward computers, the possible unemployment caused by computers, the effect of computers on privacy and freedom, computer crime, the electronic transfer of funds, and issues regarding software. These topics will be discussed in this chapter.

NEGATIVE ATTITUDES TOWARD COMPUTERS

Computers are used every day for a multitude of tasks. However, some 2
people who use computers do not understand them; others are even afraid of them. Negative attitudes toward computers may be caused by the belief that computers are smarter than people. In fact, many people do not think of computers as inhuman machines, but rather, consider them to be almost human beings. People look at the many things computers can do and fear that these machines might one day replace them and take over the world. Due to this fear of computers, many people quickly blame computers if something goes wrong. For example, imagine a situation where one person receives a million dollars in a paycheck, and another receives only one dollar. Instead of drawing the conclusion that the problem had been caused by a human error—incorrect input, for example,—most people would automatically think the computer had made the mistake.

The computer may be viewed as a "monster" by many workers who fear that they will be replaced by machines.

COMPUTERS AND UNEMPLOYMENT

The fear of computers extends to many different areas in everyday life. The computer may be viewed as a "monster" by many workers who are afraid that they will lose their jobs and be replaced by machines. Since the computer can perform many jobs automatically and does not need to take vacations or time off, many employers prefer to utilize computers rather than employ people. However, the use of robots, machines that can perform many complex jobs, and other automated procedures in business (see illustration 4.1), does not mean that people will be replaced in industry. In fact, in many cases, the jobs that are now performed by computers and robots are jobs that are tedious, boring, and disliked by workers. These workers may be retrained and learn newer and more valuable job skills. 3

COMPUTERS AND LOSS OF PRIVACY

The issue of unemployment and displacement of workers by computers and robots is only one area of concern and controversy regarding computers today. Other problematic areas concern the issue of privacy and the individual's possible loss of freedom due to computers. The issue of personal freedom is important because computers can collect and store a great deal of information about people. If an individual's rights are not protected and if careful watch is not kept over this information, it is possible that information may be illegally obtained and misused. 4

Information about individuals is currently held in auxiliary storage devices in large computer facilities. This type of computer storage, which creates a "bank" of information, is called a *data bank*. There are many data banks in existence both in the United States and abroad. Some of these data banks include those kept by the Veterans Administration (VA), which stores information about veterans of military service and their families, the Department of Transportation (DOT), which keeps records on pilots, and airplane and boat owners, and the Department of Motor Vehicles (DMV), which has information about drivers and motor vehicles. In fact, many aspects of our everyday lives including our names, marital status, income level, crime record, and credit rating are stored in various data banks. At the present time all the available information is stored in separate data banks. Since the 1970s there has been much discussion about creating a national data bank which would combine all this information in one central computer. Thus all the information about a person's life—past and present—could be accessed on a moment's notice. If such a national data bank were created, people would be assigned a personal identification number, not unlike the current United States social security number, that would be theirs from the moment of birth until death. 5

4-1 In fact, the jobs that are now performed by computers and robots are often tedious, boring, and disliked by workers.

The concept of a national data bank has always been a controversial issue. Therefore, such a central bank has never been created. Critics of this type of system point out that should such a bank be created, the potential for the unauthorized use of information is very great. It is very frightening to think that with a central data bank, almost anyone could have access to personal information about another's life almost instantaneously. It is even more upsetting to consider that this information could be used in a manner harmful to an individual, that is, for illegal or unethical purposes. In addition, if a central data bank were created, it would be very important to ensure the safety and security of the information, to guard against its misuse, and to guarantee personal freedom. 6

COMPUTER CRIME

Computer crime is another problematic area involving computers today. 7
It is difficult to determine what a computer crime is because there is no clear legal definition of what constitutes such a crime. In fact, although

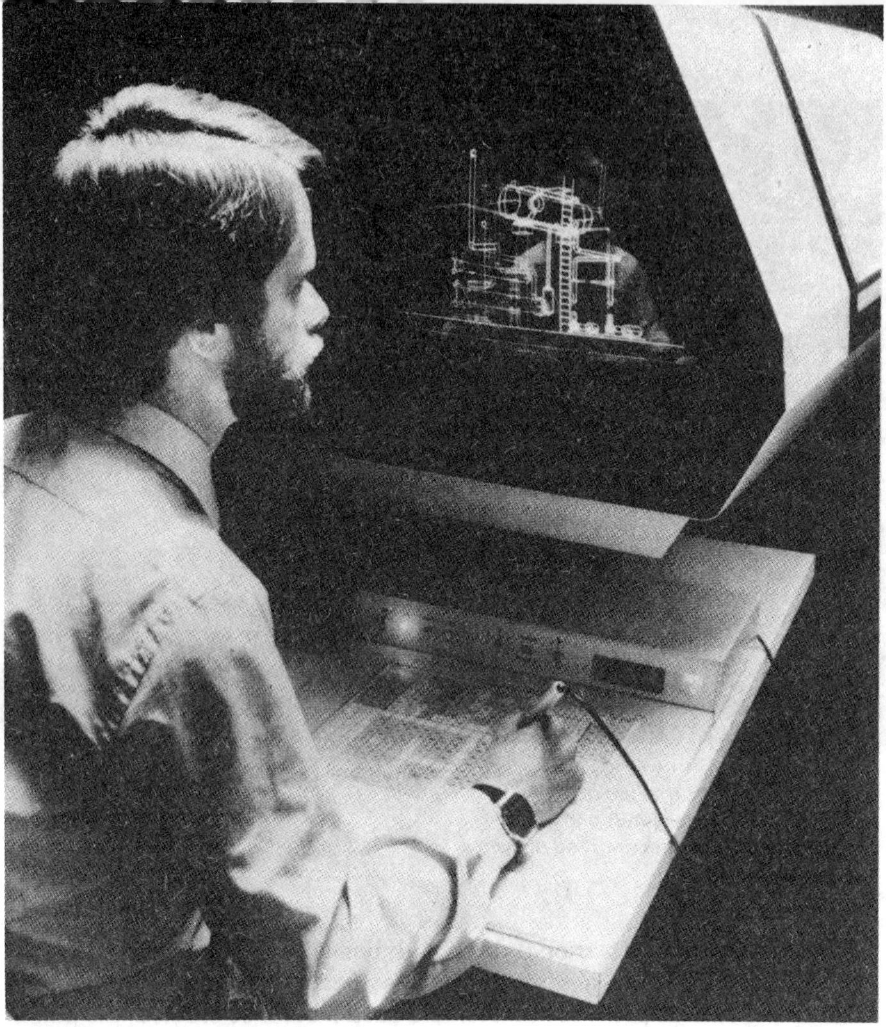

4-2 Access to specific computer systems for unauthorized activities may be considered a computer crime.

individual countries or states in the U.S. may have laws stating that certain types of computer activities are criminal, these laws are not uniform and vary a great deal. Moreover, computer technology is increasing so rapidly that new "crimes" are being invented every day.

In general, there are several types of activities involving computers 8
which may be considered crimes. One such activity is that of simple theft. This involves the physical theft of supplies such as computer paper. Another activity that may be considered a crime is the theft of computer time. This generally involves running any type of unauthorized program on a company computer. However, because the term "unauthorized programs" is so vague, this type of computer crime could include anything

from playing games to stealing important or secret data. Another crime might be the use of a computer to create false or misleading data in order to alter a particular project of another individual or company. Also included in the area of computer crime is the unauthorized access to specific computer systems by people looking for enjoyment or challenges. This type of activity is becoming more common as greater numbers of people become proficient, that is, expert, in the workings of computers. In fact, there is a special term, *hacker,* to describe those individuals who are not only very knowledgeable about computers, but spend as much time as possible working with them. Sometimes these people use their computers for some of the illegal activities described above (see illustration 4.2).

THE ELECTRONIC TRANSFER OF FUNDS: THE "CASHLESS–CHECKLESS" SOCIETY

Another area of controversy brought about by the important role of computers in modern life is that of the "cashless–checkless" society. The idea of a cashless–checkless society involves the electronic transfer of funds. All types of monetary transactions—payments, purchases, etc.—would take place electronically, without money ever being handled. This would make checks, cash, and even credit cards unnecessary. In a "cashless–checkless" society everyone would have a personal cash card, a kind of individual identification card which would be used in all types of transactions that currently call for the use of money, checks, credit cards, etc. Some people think the "cashless–checkless" society is a wonderful idea. Others point out that such a system would need a great deal of protection against crime and fraud. Security systems would have to be devised to ensure that only authorized individuals have access to specific accounts. Measures would also have to be taken to ensure that the detailed information created by all transactions could not be used for damaging purposes by either individuals or governments. 9

PROBLEMS INVOLVING SOFTWARE

Still another area of concern in regard to computers is that of software. 10
Until recently, the technological development of newer and better hardware was of major importance in the data processing field. Today technological advances in hardware are so great that the computer industry does not have enough software, or the right type of software, to take advantage of these improvements. Thus the great demand in the computer field today is not for hardware, but rather software to run on new and improved systems (see illustration 4.3).

Besides the lack of software, many of the programs that are available 11
today are unreliable. Software which contains mistakes can be very

annoying; these programs can also be very dangerous. The seriousness of computer programs which are not error-free can be shown by the systems used in space flights. Here one small mistake can not only have a negative effect on a flight, but more importantly, put lives in jeopardy. As the reliability of software, such as programs used to run modern subway systems, may affect public safety, some people feel that computer professionals should be licensed. This would require all computer professionals to pass specific exams before being allowed to work. Some people also feel that those involved in the computer field should carry insurance and be legally responsible for the mistakes in their programs which might harm the general population.

COMPUTER PIRACY

Another aspect of the controversy involving software is that of computer piracy—the unlawful copying or duplication of software. It is currently common and often very easy for people to make copies of computer software instead of buying it. The issue of pirating computer software by copying it is related to the problem of obtaining legal protection for computer programs. Such protection may be in the form of a copyright, a means to ensure that the author or creator of a specific item is given the exclusive legal right to that item. It is very difficult to stop the pirating of computer software because many laws regarding the copyrighting of software are not clear. It is currently possible to copyright certain aspects of computer programs. However, the issue of proving ownership of the logic and basic structure of a program is still unresolved. Thus, while it is technically illegal to copy a specific program, it is impossible to stop others from copying or modifying its logic and structural composition. 12

SUMMARY

Due to computers, our lives have changed very much and will continue to change in the future. Although only some of the problematic areas concerning computers have been mentioned briefly in this chapter, ethical and sensible resolution of these problems, and consistent control and coordination of computers, are essential for a healthy society. 13

EXERCISES

Vocabulary from Context

A. Choose the letter of the word or expression that is closest in meaning to the first word or words. Refer to the indicated paragraph as necessary.

1. robots (3)
   a. human beings
   b. machines that do many complex tasks
   c. machines that think like people
2. privacy (4)
   a. loss of personal freedom
   b. information about freedom stored in data banks
   c. the right to personal freedom
3. data bank (5)
   a. a large collection of information
   b. a foreign bank
   c. information about banks
4. electronic transfer of funds (9)
   a. using electronic money
   b. using checks instead of money
   c. making financial transactions electronically
5. copyright (12)
   a. the right to make copies of computer programs
   b. legal rights
   c. legal and exclusive ownership of a product or creation
6. piracy (12)
   a. stealing computers
   b. unauthorized duplication of programs
   c. authorized duplication of programs

B. Fill in the blanks with one of the following words or terms from the reading. Refer to the indicated paragraph as necessary. Be sure to use the correct grammatical form.

prominent (1)	multitude (2)	to blame (2)
tedious (3)	controversial (6)	to guarantee (6)
uniform (7)	vague (8)	proficient (8)
jeopardy (11)	exclusive (12)	

1. Many jobs are performed by computers; they carry out a _____of tasks.
2. Computers, due to their importance in society, play a _____ role in modern life.
3. Protection is needed to guard against illegal use of information so that we can _____ personal freedom and privacy.
4. Computers are not responsible for mistakes in programs; people are. However, it is common to place the responsibility for errors on the computer and _____ it for problems.

5. Sometimes unreliable software can be dangerous and put people in ____.
6. Some jobs are repetitive and boring. They may be ____ for people, but not for machines.
7. Some people want to create a national data bank; others think it is a very bad idea. The creation of a central data bank is a very ____ issue.
8. The definition of computer crime is unclear and ____.
9. The laws defining computer crime are not ____, but are different in every state and country.
10. In order to be the only owner of program it is necessary to legally obtain ____ rights to the program.
11. More and more people are becoming ____ in the workings of computers; indeed, there is a growing number of computer experts in today's society.

C. Find each of the following words or terms in the indicated paragraph in the reading. Then write a synonym, definition, or description of the word or term. Use your dictionary only if necessary.

1. abroad (5)
2. monetary (9)
3. reliability (11)
4. duplication (12)

D. Write the acronyms for the following.

1. Department of Transportation
2. Veterans Administration
3. Department of Motor Vehicles

Comprehension Exercises

A. True-False. Write a "T" if the statement is true. Write "F" if it is false.

1. Some people think that computers might someday replace them and take over the world.
2. In the future, all jobs will be done by computers and robots.
3. Great amounts of information are currently being stored in data banks.
4. A national data bank exists today.
5. People fear that information collected by computers might be used wrongly.
6. There is no clear definition of computer crime.
7. With electronic funds transfer, money is carried by messengers.

8. The development of computer software is currently not keeping up with the demand for it.
9. Computer professionals must presently be licensed in order to work.
10. Modern society has strict and consistent laws regarding the copyrighting of computer programs.
11. Unauthorized duplication of programs is a problem in society.

B. Choose the letter of the *best* answer for each of the following.

1. According to the reading, what is *not* true about people who dislike computers?
   a. People think that computers are smarter than they are.
   b. People think that computers will take their jobs.
   c. People think that computers only give pennies in paychecks.
   d. People think that computers are responsible for many problems.

2. People who lose their jobs to computers ____.
   a. take too many vacations
   b. like computers
   c. perform jobs automatically
   d. may be retrained

3. Computers can cause the loss of privacy if ____.
   a. they collect information
   b. the information is not used correctly
   c. the information is in a data bank
   d. a bad credit rating is stored in a data bank

4. A central data bank ____.
   a. would be a national facility containing all available information about individuals
   b. would guarantee the individual's personal freedom
   c. would contain only information about an individual's past
   d. will be created soon

5. The idea of computer crime, as explained in this chapter, includes all the following except ____.
   a. the theft of computer supplies
   b. unauthorized access to private systems
   c. the creation of misleading data
   d. the development of authorized programs

6. What would *not* be a characteristic of a cashless–checkless society?
   a. the absence of money
   b. paying for bills electronically
   c. making change
   d. using a personal cash card

7. Current issues concerning software do *not* include ____.
   a. software reliability
   b. protecting the public from errors in programs
   c. possible licensing of computer professionals
   d. creating new computer languages

Skill Enhancement

Restatement and Inference

When we read something, we understand and interpret the information in different ways. We may find one idea expressed in several different ways. We may be able to draw conclusions based on what we can infer from a reading passage.

Another way of stating the same information already expressed in the paragraph is *restatement.* It is a paraphrase of the original statement; it is the original statement expressed in a different form.

Example: (original sentence) Many people are afraid of computers.
(restatement) Computers scare large numbers of people.

Conclusions that the reader can draw from the information expressed in the paragraph are *inferences.* The conclusion is not stated; the reader must use what he or she understands from the reading to arrive at a conclusion.

4-3 The great demand in the computer field today is not for hardware, but rather software to run on new and improved systems.

Example: (original sentence) In the future, it is likely that large numbers of people will work at home.
(inference) Changes in people's working habits will be brought about by computers.

Statements which are not true based on the information in the paragraph are *wrong*.

Example: (original sentence) In the future all types of printed materials will be available on computers.
(wrong statement) Books will never be put on computers.

Statements which cannot be proven true or false based on the information in the reading can be called *unproven*. The reader cannot judge the truth of the sentence because the information supporting or contradicting it is simply not there.

Example: (original sentence) Two controversial areas regarding computers are privacy and unemployment.
(unproven statement) Piracy is a controversial area concerning computers.

Read the following paragraphs and then decide what type of statement each sentence is in relation to the information in the original paragraph. Use the following system of notation:

Use **R** if the statement is a restatement of the information in the paragraph.
Use **I** if the statement is an inference about information in the paragraph.
Use **W** if the statement is wrong according to the paragraph.
Use **U** if the statement cannot be proven from information in the paragraph.

There may be more than one statement of a particular type in each example. Two examples from the first paragraph have been done for you.

A. Many people use computers every day for a variety of tasks. However, some people who use computers do not understand them; others are even afraid of them. Negative attitudes toward computers may be caused by the general belief that computers are smarter than people. In fact, many people do not think of computers as inhuman machines, but rather, consider them to be almost human beings. People look at the many things computers can do and fear that they will one day replace mankind and take over the world. Due to this fear of computers, many people quickly blame computers if something goes wrong. Instead of examining the situation and drawing the conclusion that the problem has been caused by a human error, most people automatically blame the computer.

Sample Answers

1. R Computers are used for many different jobs on a daily basis. This is a restatement of the first sentence. A variety (many kinds) of jobs are performed every day (on a daily basis) by computers.
2. I Some people dislike computers because of what they think are the machines' superior capabilities.
   This can be inferred from the paragraph. We can infer that people dislike computers because they think the machines are superior to them.

Decide what kind of statement each sentence is, based on the paragraph above.

1. ____ Some people attribute almost human qualities to computers.
2. ____ If people would analyze situations in which mistakes have been blamed on computers, they would realize that the error was caused by a person and not a computer.
3. ____ Seventy-five percent of the population of the U.S. uses computers.
4. ____ Computers are very often blamed for mistakes made by people.
5. ____ People are always 100% correct.

B. The computer is sometimes viewed as a "monster" by many workers who are afraid that they will lose their jobs and be replaced by machines. Since the computer can perform many jobs automatically and does not need to take vacations or time off, many employers prefer to utilize computers rather than employ people. However, the use of automated procedures in business, and more recently robots, machines that may look like human beings and can perform many complex human activities, does not mean that people will lose their jobs and never work again. In fact, often the jobs that are now performed by computers and robots are jobs that are tedious, boring and disliked by workers. These workers may be retrained and learn newer and more valuable job skills.

1. ____ Robots can perform some of the same jobs as people.
2. ____ Some of the jobs now performed by machines are routine tasks which people like very much.
3. ____ Computers are used to announce important information.
4. ____ Robots were introduced into business after other types of machines.
5. ____ Robots, computers and other machines can be beneficial both to employers and employees.

C. The concept of a national data bank has always been a controversial issue. Therefore, such a centralized bank has never been created. Critics of the system point out that the potential for unauthorized use of information is very great. It is very frightening to think that almost anyone could have access to all the information about your life in a short time. It is even more frightening to think that this information might be used for illegal or unethical purposes. In addition, if a central data bank were created, plans would have to be made to ensure the safety and security of the information, to guard against its misuse and to guarantee personal freedom.

1. _____ Protecting a person's privacy is important.
2. _____ People are not at all afraid of the idea of a national data bank.
3. _____ All information in all types of data banks can be used for dangerous purposes.
4. _____ A national data bank would have been created if the concept had not been so controversial.
5. _____ Using information in such a way as to take away man's freedom and privacy is wrong.

D. The seriousness of computer programs which are not error-free can be exemplified by the systems used in space flights. Here one small mistake can not only have a negative effect on the flight, but, more importantly, put lives in jeopardy. As the reliability of software may often affect the public safety, some people feel that all computer professionals, like doctors or lawyers, should be licensed. Some people also feel that those involved in the computer field should carry insurance and be legally responsible for the mistakes in their programs which might harm the general population.

1. _____ Human lives are more important than space missions.
2. _____ Computer professionals are now legally responsible for their programs.
3. _____ There should be no mistakes in the programs used in the space program.
4. _____ Insurance is expensive.
5. _____ According to some people, a license should be required of all computer professionals.

Enrichment Activities

1. Select several paragraphs from the chapter and write sentences which are restatements of the information. Then write sentences making inferences from the information in the paragraph.

2. Prepare an oral or written report on a current issue involving computers in modern society.

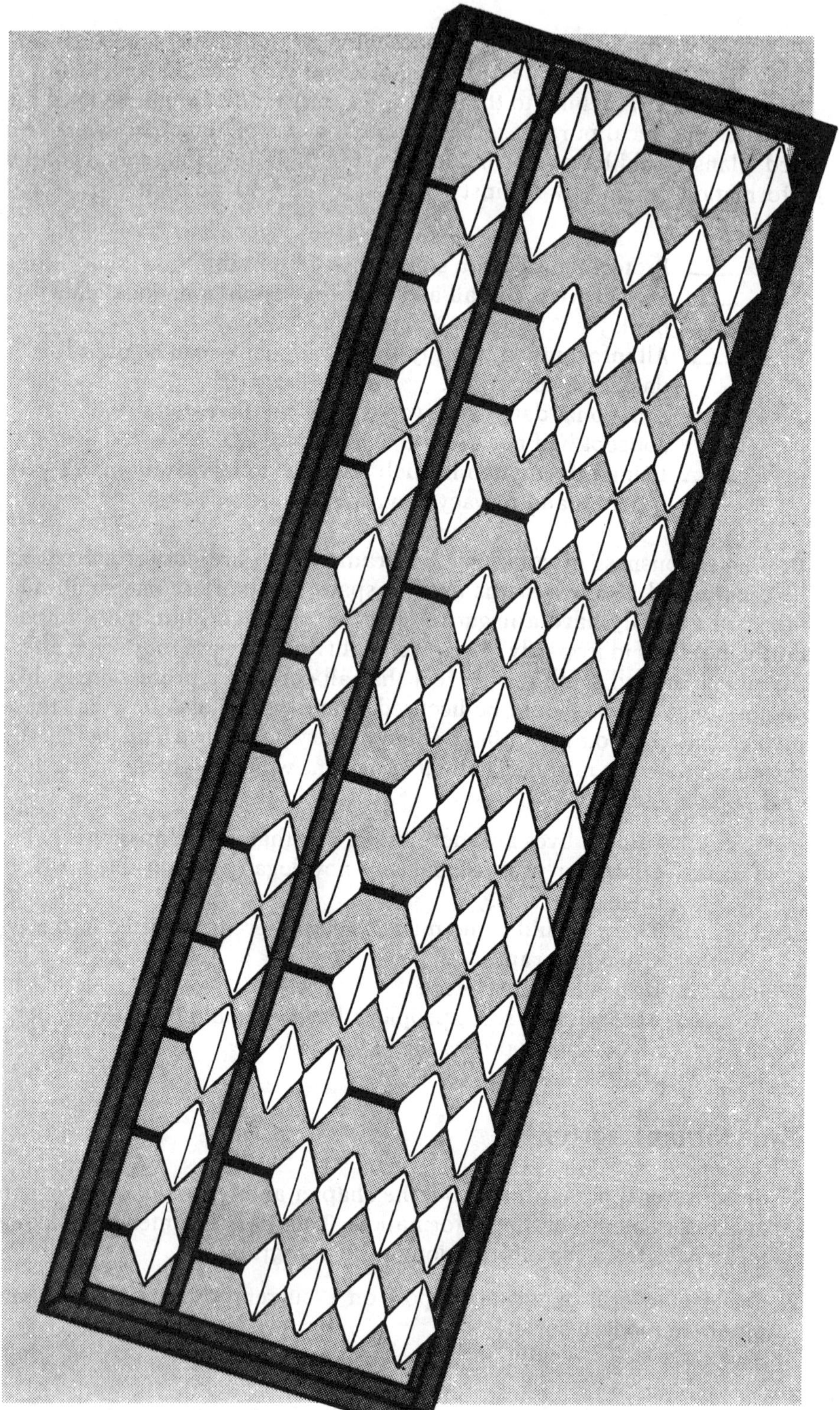

CHAPTER 5

HISTORY OF COMPUTERS: PART I

The modern computer would not exist without the research and inven- 1
tions of the past. For this reason, it is very useful to become familiar with the evolution of the computer. This history of the development of the computer includes all the advances made prior to the development of the device itself. Studying this material will help you understand the impact, or effect, of computers on technology and society.

EARLY DEVELOPMENTS

One of the first devices used by man to process data was the *abacus*. The 2
abacus (the plural of which is *abaci*) is a device used to perform calculations by moving counters which are made of small beads or stones. These counters are moved up and down on a string or a wire (see illustration 5.1). Abaci are, therefore, also referred to as counting boards. This tool, which was used in ancient times, is still used today to make arithmetical computations.

Centuries after the invention of the abacus, during the period called 3
the Scientific Revolution, which began around 1540 and culminated in 1687, scientists invented other computational devices. The Scientific Revolution was an important period because people began to pay more attention to science in general. To begin with, in 1642, Blaise Pascal, a French mathematician, invented the first mechanical calculator (see illustration 5.2). Then, in 1673, Gottfried von Leibnitz, a German mathematician, invented another calculating machine. Pascal and Leibnitz both understood that machines could help mathematicians and businessmen save time and money. In fact, both men tried to sell their inventions to busi-

5-1 One of the first devices used by man to process data was the abacus. Abaci are also referred to as counting boards.

nesses. Following the development of these first, fairly simple, calculating machines, more complex devices were invented.

The Scientific Revolution prepared the way for the great technologi- 4
cal advances of the Industrial Revolution. The Industrial Revolution started in England after the end of the Scientific Revolution. It caused major societal and technological changes which spread to other countries in Europe and to the United States. Society was affected in several ways. To begin with, people moved from the farms to the cities in order to get jobs. This meant that society became urban rather than rural. Furthermore, most products were made by machine instead of by hand. This mechanization of businesses meant that fewer people could make more, and sometimes better, products. Following that development, people became distrustful of machines. (Many people today feel this way about computers.) Finally, an entire new class, or group, of working people became an important part of society.

THE INDUSTRIAL REVOLUTION

The Industrial Revolution also brought advances in technology. Several 5
machines which later had an impact on the development of the computer were developed. First, in 1804, a Frenchman named Joseph Marie Jacquard invented a new weaving loom (a machine to make cloth). This loom was "programmed" to make certain patterns, that is, pictures or designs.

5-2 The first mechanical calculator, invented in 1642 by Blaise Pascal, a French mathematician.

Jacquard accomplished this by punching holes in paper cards according to a code. This machine was the forerunner of the punched-card devices which will be studied later (see below).

After that, in 1822, an Englishman named Charles Babbage made 6
some important advances in technology. First, in 1822, Babbage built an enormous machine which he called the *difference engine* (see illustration 5.3). This device could figure mathematical tables. Next, in 1833, he envisioned a machine which could complete programmed arithmetic opera-

The Jacquard loom was "programmed" to make patterns through the use of punched paper cards.

5-3 The difference engine, invented by Charles Babbage in 1822, was capable of performing arithmetic operations.

tions (addition, subtraction, multiplication, and division). He also imagined that the machine might be able to store, or remember, the results. He called this machine the *analytical engine.* Unfortunately, the technology during Babbage's lifetime was not sufficiently developed and his dream was never realized. Although Babbage's dream did not come true at that time, his ideas were eventually used in making the modern computer.

While Babbage was developing his ideas for the difference and ana- 7
lytical engines, his friend, Lady Ada Lovelace, daughter of the famous poet Lord Byron, was also hard at work. As a mathematician, Lady Lovelace invented an arithmetic code for Babbage's machine. This code, like modern codes used with computers, was based on a *binary* (having two numbers) number system. For this reason, Lady Lovelace is often called the first programmer. Furthermore, as a tribute to Lady Lovelace's role in the history of computers, the U.S. Department of Defense has named a programming language after her. It is called "Ada."

FROM THE INDUSTRIAL REVOLUTION TO THE FIRST MODERN COMPUTER

After the Industrial Revolution, most advances in the development of the 8
computer took place in the United States. The first significant developments in the history of computers in the U.S. were made by a man named Herman Hollerith. Dr. Hollerith worked for the U.S. Bureau of the Census, the agency that keeps information on the population. Because the 1880 census count was not truly complete until 1889, it was clear that census reports could not be up-to-date. First, in the late 1880s, Dr. Hollerith developed a card that had coded data in punched holes. Then he invented

machines which could read these data and process them. For example, one machine sorted, or separated the cards; another machine tabulated, or counted, numbers; and still another merged, or joined, two sets of punched cards. As a result of these inventions, the 1890 census took only two and a half years to tabulate. A few years afterward, Hollerith started the Tabulating Machine Company in order to manufacture his devices. Subsequently, this company became part of the world-famous company called IBM (International Business Machines).

During the years succeeding Hollerith's inventions, both the punched card and the machines used with it were improved. The improved machines were called EAM (*E*lectrical *A*ccounting *M*achines) devices. The punched cards and the machines based on Hollerith's inventions are not used very frequently today. 9

Later, certain problems with the punched card and the accounting machines developed. First, because the machines were mechanical (operating with gears and levers), their speed was limited. Second, since each machine performed a different job, extra time was needed to change the cards from one machine to another. Last, and above all, the possibility for mistakes was high because of the need to keep transferring the cards. 10

During the Second World War the modern age of computers began with the development of the first electronic computers. Several developments took place during this period of time which changed the history of computation. 11

1. 1938–1942. Professor John V. Atanasoff of Iowa State College and his assistant, Clifford Berry, designed and built the Atanasoff-Berry computer, the ABC. It was the first electronic digital computer and provided the basis for the development of the ENIAC.
2. 1939–1944. Professor Howard Aiken of Harvard University, together with some engineers from IBM, built an enormous calculating machine. This joint effort produced the MARK 1, an electro-mechanical device that was controlled by punched cards. MARK 1 was used in military ballistics (the study of the motion of bullets, missiles, bombs, etc.).
3. 1943–1946. Dr. John W. Mauchly and J. Presper Eckert, with funding from the U.S. Army, constructed the ENIAC (*E*lectronic *N*umerical *I*ntegrator and *C*omputer). This was the first major electronic digital computer. The ENIAC was an enormous machine which weighed about 30 tons (1 ton = 2,000 pounds) and took up an area of 1,500 square feet (see illustration 5-4). The ENIAC is particularly important in the history of computers because it provided the basis of modern computer technology.

The developments which took place during World War II led to the important advances made in the period after the war. This period can be referred to as the modern age of computers. We will study the developments which have taken place during this time in the following chapter. 12

5-4 The ENIAC, the first major electronic digital computer, was an enormous machine that weighed 30 tons and took up an area of 1,500 square feet.

EXERCISES

Vocabulary from Context

A. Choose the letter of the word or expression that is closest in meaning to the first word or words. Refer to the indicated paragraph as necessary.

1. complex (3)
   a. complete
   b. not simple
   c. not complicated
2. urban (4)
   a. of the city
   b. of the country
   c. of the suburbs
3. rural (4)
   a. of the city
   b. of the country
   c. of the suburbs
4. loom (5)
   a. a punched-card machine
   b. a computer
   c. a machine to make cloth
5. to store (6)
   a. to remember
   b. to sell
   c. to calculate
6. sufficiently (6)
   a. soon
   b. enough
   c. ready
7. up-to-date (8)
   a. recent
   b. old
   c. fast
8. to merge (8)
   a. to join
   b. to count
   c. to sort
9. to transfer (10)
   a. to change from one to another
   b. to set up
   c. to lose time
10. funding (11)
    a. taxes
    b. scientific help
    c. financial aid
11. joint (11)
    a. combined
    b. try
    c. productive

B. Fill in the blanks with one of the following words or terms from the reading. Refer to the indicated paragraph as necessary. Be sure to use the correct grammatical form.

evolution (1)	device (2)	computation (2)
to culminate (3)	forerunner (5)	operations (6)
significant (8)	to sort (8)	to tabulate (8)

1. Addition, subtraction, multiplication, and division are examples of mathematical _____.

2. It would be difficult ____ the census without computers. Counting large populations requires advanced technology.
3. The ABC was built before the ENIAC. The ABC was the ____ of the ENIAC.
4. When we study the ____ of computers, we study the history of their development.
5. When doing the laundry, you should separate the dark clothes from the white clothes. If you don't ____ them this way, the colors may run.
6. It would be impossible to do long calculations as fast as a computer. Complicated ____ should be left to the machine.
7. World War II began in 1939 and ____ in 1945.
8. A ____ is a tool or machine which we use to help us.
9. Important developments in the world should be studied carefully. Such ____ happenings affect everyone.

C. Find each of the following words or terms in the indicated paragraph in the reading. Then write a synonym, definition, or description of the word or term. Use your dictionary only if necessary.

1. abacus (2)
2. mechanization (4)
3. tribute (7)
4. mechanical (10)
5. ballistics (11)

Comprehension Exercises

A. True-False. Write a "T" if the statement is true. Write "F" if it is false.

1. The ENIAC preceded the ABC.
2. The abacus is still in use today.
3. There were no calculating machines before the 1890 census.
4. The MARK 1 was used to tabulate the census.
5. Herman Hollerith made many contributions to the development of the modern computer.

B. Choose the letter of the *best* answer for each of the following.

1. Studying the history of computers will help you understand ____
   a. evolution
   b. society
   c. technology
   d. the impact of computers on society and technology

2. The abacus is used ____.
   a. to tabulate the census
   b. for military ballistics
   c. to perform mathematical computations
   d. only in museums

3. Early calculating machines were invented by ____.
   a. Joseph Jacquard and Charles Babbage
   b. J. Presper Eckert and John W. Mauchly
   c. John V. Atanasoff and Clifford Berry
   d. Blaise Pascal and Gottfried Leibnitz

4. Which of the following is *not* a change caused by the Industrial Revolution?
   a. everyone began to accept machines
   b. society became urban rather than rural
   c. industry was mechanized
   d. a new class of working people was created

5. Why is Jacquard's loom important in the evolution of computers?
   a. because it made better cloth
   b. because it was the forerunner of punched-card machines
   c. because it led to the analytical engine
   d. because it was invented during the Industrial Revolution

6. Charles Babbage is important because ____.
   a. he knew Lord Byron's daughter
   b. his ideas became part of the modern computer
   c. he built the analytical engine
   d. the difference engine could make mathematical tables

7. Who invented the punched card and a code for using it?
   a. Babbage
   b. Leibnitz
   c. Hollerith
   d. Mauchly

8. Which of the following was *not* a problem with the machines used with punched cards?
   a. the technology was not advanced enough to use them correctly
   b. they operated at limited speeds
   c. transferring cards caused a loss of time
   d. the possibility for error was high

9. Which development in the evolution of computers did *not* occur during World War II?
   a. the Atanasoff-Berry Computer
   b. the punched card

c. the MARK 1
d. the ENIAC

10. Which of the following best describes the ENIAC?
    a. It was a mechanical device.
    b. It was designed in a joint effort with IBM engineers.
    c. It was used to compute tables for military ballistics.
    d. It provided the basis of modern computer technology.

Skill Enhancement

Paragraphs are often structured by means of a sequence. That sequence can follow several different kinds of order:

1. Chronological (time) order indicates the order in which events happen. The chronological description of a process describes *how* something happens from beginning to end.
2. Order of importance indicates events or elements according to their importance:
   a. ascending order proceeds from the *least* important to the *most* important item
   b. descending order proceeds from the *most* important to the *least* important item.
3. Enumeration or listing is a way to describe events or elements without special regard to importance or time.

Sequence markers are words or phrases that indicate the use of sequential ordering within a paragraph. These words can introduce either the beginning, middle, or end of a sequence. Following is a list of sequence markers and the position in which they may appear:

Beginning	**Middle**		**Final**
first	then	further	finally
firstly	next	furthermore	lastly
in the first place	after that	subsequently	above all
initially	afterward	succeeding	last, but not least
to begin with	later	two (2), etc.*	eventually
to start with	following		
one (1)*			

*Cardinal numbers (see Chapter 10) are useful in listing items, particularly in scientific and technical writing.

Skill Exercise

Example: In the third paragraph, the first sequence marker is "after" in the sentence beginning "Centuries after the invention of the abacus. . . ." There are 3 other sequence markers in this sentence. They are:

1. to begin with
2. then
3. following

Which kind of sequence do these markers indicate? (Check all that apply.)

1. chronological order
2. ascending order of importance
3. descending order of importance
4. enumeration or listing

The sequence described in this paragraph is chronological because it describes events in the order in which they happened. There are no other sequences in this paragraph.

1. Paragraph 4 has four sequence markers. The first one, "after," links the paragraph by time to the previous one. List the other sequence markers as they appear in the paragraph.

1. ____________________
2. ____________________
3. ____________________
4. ____________________

Which kind of sequence do these markers indicate? (Check all that apply.)

1. chronological order
2. ascending order of importance
3. descending order of importance
4. enumeration or listing

Explain why you chose the answer you did.

2. Paragraph 9 has four sequence markers. List them as they appear in the paragraph.

1. ____________________
2. ____________________
3. ____________________
4. ____________________

Which kind of sequence do these markers indicate? (Check all that apply.)

1. chronological order
2. ascending order of importance
3. descending order of importance
4. enumeration or listing

Explain why you chose the answer you did.

3. Paragraph 11 has five sequence markers. List them as they appear in the paragraph.

1. ____________________
2. ____________________
3. ____________________
4. ____________________
5. ____________________

Which kind of sequence do these markers indicate? (Check all that apply.)

1. chronological order
2. ascending order of importance
3. descending order of importance
4. enumeration or listing

Explain why you chose the answer you did.

4. How many sequence markers does paragraph 12 have? List them as they appear in the paragraph.

____

____

____

____

Which kind of sequence do these markers indicate? (Check all that apply.)

1. chronological order
2. ascending order of importance
3. descending order of importance
4. enumeration or listing

Explain why you chose the answer you did.

Enrichment Activities

1. Write a paragraph using sequence markers and the following information. Use any of the sequence types studied in this lesson, but be sure to use only one type.

   Dr. John V. Atanasoff taught mathematics at Iowa State College.
   Atanasoff wanted a machine to perform calculations for his graduate students.
   He tried to design a machine, but could not complete it.
   His assistant, Clifford Berry, helped him finish the design.
   Together the two men built the Atanasoff-Berry Computer.
   The ABC was really the first electronic digital computer.

2. Discuss the importance of knowing the history of advances in science and technology. Appoint or elect a group spokesperson to present the group's conclusions to the class.

3. Visit an exhibit at a local museum or institution (university, technical society, etc.) that shows the history of a development in a scientific or technological field. Tell the class about your visit. Be sure to show the class any printed information that you may have gotten at the exhibit.

CHAPTER

6

HISTORY OF COMPUTERS: PART II

Although many important developments in computer technology had 1
taken place before the end of World War II, in the period after the war, major new advances in the history of technology took place. In fact, these unequalled developments in computer technology have occurred only since 1945. The computer industry itself has changed radically within that short span of time as well.

THE FIRST GENERATION

Near the end of World War II, Dr. John von Neumann developed what we 2
refer to as the *stored program concept*. Prior to this development, in computers like the ENIAC, thousands of switches had to be changed by hand each time a new program was needed. In the computers using the stored program concept, the computer was directly controlled by a program kept in the machine instead of being controlled by the manual changing of wires. This stored program concept revolutionized the computer industry. Designers have been using the stored program concept in building digital computers ever since von Neumann first explained his theory.

While von Neumann was working with Eckert and Mauchly at the 3
University of Pennsylvania, Maurice V. Wilkes was attending classes there. When Wilkes returned to Cambridge University in England, he brought the idea of the stored program with him. He began to work on the EDSAC (*E*lectronic *D*elay *S*torage *A*utomatic *C*alculator) and completed it in 1949. The EDSAC, the first stored program computer, had been working for approximately two years when Mauchly and Eckert finished their stored program computer, the EDVAC (*E*lectronic *D*iscrete *V*ariable *A*utomatic *C*omputer) in 1951.

Computers are used in the field of health care for various purposes. Administrative duties are often performed by the computer.

While they were working on the EDVAC, Mauchly and Eckert formed 4
their own computer company. In 1950, the Remington–Rand Corporation (which later became Sperry–Rand) took over their company. In 1951, after Remington–Rand got control of the company, the first commercial computer, the UNIVAC (*UNIV*ersal *A*utomatic *C*omputer) was delivered to the U.S. Census Bureau. Although Remington–Rand had entered the computer manufacturing business by the early 1950s, another company soon replaced it as the leader in the field. By 1956, IBM had become the largest computer company. It has been the leading U.S. computer manufacturer since that time.

The U.S. government had been using the UNIVAC for more than a 5
year when, in 1952, people using the computer correctly predicted the outcome of the presidential election. After the UNIVAC had analyzed only 5% of the vote, it was predicted that Dwight D. Eisenhower would win the election. By the time all the votes were counted, the UNIVAC's operators had known the probable results for many hours. That was the first time in the history of technology that a computer performed such a task. Today, it is common for people to use computers for such a purpose. In fact, computers have been used to predict the outcome of U.S. presidential elections for more than 30 years.

These early computers are known as first generation computers. They 6
used vacuum tubes to control their operations. However, there were several problems associated with, or related to, the use of vacuum tubes. First, because the tubes themselves were fairly large and thousands of them were needed to build the machine, the computer took up a tremendous amount of space. Second, computers made with vacuum tubes used a great deal of power and, for that reason, gave off a great deal of heat. Because the computers generated so much heat, computer areas had to have very good air conditioning. Third, these huge computers could be unreliable. People could not always depend on them because they often broke down. These devices required a great deal of maintenance, or upkeep and repair. Fourth, in addition to sometimes being undependable, these first generation computers were somewhat slow. Finally, the memory space where programs could be stored was relatively small. For all these reasons, it was clear to both scientists and computer users that further technological advances were needed.

Due to the fact that computers only understood a special binary code 7
(which we will study in Chapter 10), programming them was a very time-consuming job. Not only did this task require a great deal of time, but, because it was so complex, mistakes were common. In order to facilitate this task, that is, to make it easier, several people invented programs which translated symbols to the binary code that the computer could understand. In 1952, Dr. Grace Hopper developed the first of these programs. Two years later, John Backus, together with some people from IBM, began to work on another programming language. They had been working for three years when they completed the first version of the pro-

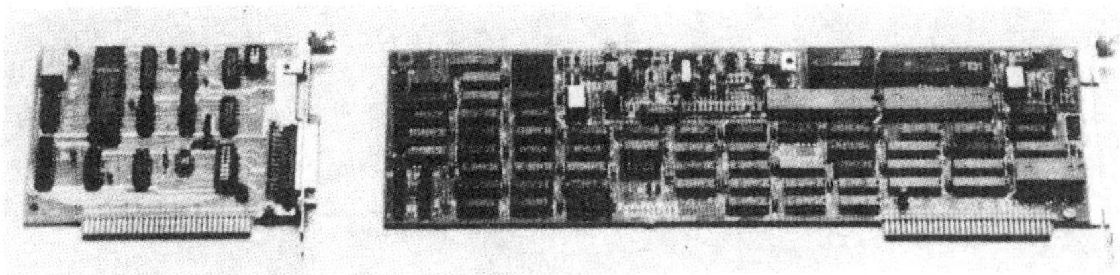

6-1 Transistors were used in computers from 1958 to 1964.

6-2 The third generation of computers began around 1965 when integrated circuits took the place of transistors.

gramming language FORTRAN (*FOR*mula *TRAN*slation). By 1959, programmers had invented more than 200 programming languages. We will study some of these in Chapter 11.

THE SECOND GENERATION

In 1947, three scientists at Bell Laboratories invented something that 8
would solve the problems of vacuum tube computers. J. Bardeen, W. H. Brattain, and W. Shockley developed the transistor (see illustration 6.1).

6-3 Large scale technology has reduced the size of the computer, making it portable, powerful, and more reliable than previous computers.

After having developed it, they won the Nobel Prize for their work. Manufacturers used transistors in computers from about 1958 to 1964. The computers that used transistors are known as second generation computers. They were smaller, faster, and more reliable than first generation computers. In addition, computers made with transistors generated less heat, cost less money, and used less power. Users programmed second generation computers with high-level programming languages, that is, languages like FORTRAN, which were closer to English.

THE THIRD GENERATION AND BEYOND

The third generation of computers began around 1965 when *i*ntegrated 9
*c*ircuits (ICs) (see illustration 6.2) took the place of transistors. Computer companies have been using integrated circuits in computers ever since 1965. Because *microchips,* the tiny boards that contain these circuits, are so small (less than ⅛ of an inch square), third generation computers are much smaller than any previous computers. These computers have also become more powerful, less expensive, faster, and more reliable than any previous computer. People depend on computers with integrated circuits every day throughout the world.

Some people call the large computers we use today the fourth gen- 10
eration of computers, because they are much smaller and much more powerful than those used in the 1960s. These machines still use integrated circuits, but these circuits are the product of *L*arge *S*cale *I*ntegration (LSI) and *V*ery *L*arge *S*cale *I*ntegration (VLSI). Such large-scale technology has reduced the size of the computer so much (see illustration 6.3) that many people feel that the computer industry has undergone another revolution. It has also made the microcomputer, the small personal computer, very common. We will learn more about the computers in use today in Chapter 9.

Due to the fact that scientists are constantly making advances in tech- 11
nology, it is likely that the pattern of past developments will continue. That is, in the future, we will probably be using computers that are smaller, faster, cheaper, more powerful, and more reliable than the ones we are using right now. Japanese scientists have begun what they refer to as the "Fifth Generation Project." Not only do they expect the computers of the fifth generation to be faster and more powerful than any previous computer, they expect these machines to be able to reason and to communicate with humans in natural language. The U.S. Department of Defense has begun similar projects in its research division DARPA (*D*efense *A*dvanced *R*esearch *P*roject *A*gency). It is expected that these projects will take us into a fifth generation of computers before the end of the century. It is probable that, by the year 2000, computer technology will have advanced so much that today's computers will be completely outdated—they will be obsolete. Although people will have been relying on computers for only about 55 years by that time, it will probably be very difficult to imagine life without these devices.

EXERCISES

Vocabulary from Context

A. Choose the letter of the word or expression that is closest in meaning to the first word or words. Refer to the indicated paragraph as necessary.

1. span of time (1)
   a. short time
   b. period of time
   c. forty years

2. prior to (2)
   a. before
   b. after
   c. during

3. to revolutionize (2)
   a. to change completely
   b. to change governments
   c. to reduce

4. outcome (5)
   a. prediction
   b. election
   c. result

5. task (5)
   a. job
   b. performance
   c. program

6. associated with (6)
   a. overcome with
   b. required to
   c. related to

7. a great deal of (6)
   a. large
   b. a lot of
   c. some

8. unreliable (6)
   a. unusual
   b. understandable
   c. undependable

9. maintenance (6)
   a. requirement
   b. machinery
   c. upkeep

10. tiny (9)
    a. very small
    b. square
    c. previous

B. Fill in the blanks with one of the following words or terms from the reading. Refer to the indicated paragraph as necessary. Be sure to use the correct grammatical form.

unequalled (1)	manual (2)	to take over (4)
tremendous (6)	to generate (6)	time-consuming (7)
to facilitate (7)	obsolete (11)	

1. An _____ event is an event which has never been matched.
2. If we refer to something as _____, we mean that it is completely out-of-date.
3. A very large machine could be called a _____ machine.
4. _____ labor is work that is done by hand.
5. After the millionaire got control of one computer company, she decided _____ another one.
6. Modern computers _____ some heat, but they don't give off as much heat as the early computers did.
7. It was necessary _____ the job of programming because it was so difficult.
8. Learning a new language is a _____ process; however, most people agree that spending so much time is worth it.

C. Find each of the following words or terms in the indicated paragraph in the reading. Then write a synonym, definition, or description of the word or term.

1. stored program concept (2)
2. EDSAC (3)
3. EDVAC (3)
4. UNIVAC (4)
5. high-level programming language (8)
6. microchip (9)

Comprehension Exercises

A. True-False. Write a "T" if the statement is true. Write "F" if it is false.

1. The stored program concept is not important in the evolution of computers.
2. The UNIVAC was controlled by the manual switching of wires.
3. The first stored program computer was built in England.

4. IBM has always been the leading manufacturer of computers.
5. The U.S. Census Bureau used the UNIVAC.

B. Choose the letter of the *best* answer for each of the following.

1. Which of the following is *not* a characteristic of first generation computers?
   a. they used vacuum tubes
   b. they fit in a small space
   c. they generated a lot of heat
   d. they could be unreliable
2. Who developed the stored program concept?
   a. Grace Hopper
   b. Maurice Wilkes
   c. John von Neumann
   d. John Backus
3. Which was the first commercial stored program computer?
   a. ENIAC
   b. EDSAC
   c. EDVAC
   d. UNIVAC
4. Who developed one of the first programs to translate symbols into a language the machine can understand?
   a. Grace Hopper
   b. John von Neumann
   c. Maurice Wilkes
   d. J. Presper Eckert
5. In what year was the first version of FORTRAN completed?
   a. 1949
   b. 1952
   c. 1954
   d. 1957
6. Which of the following scientists did *not* win the Nobel Prize for the development of the transistor?
   a. J. Bardeen
   b. J. W. Mauchly
   c. W. Shockley
   d. W. H. Brattain
7. During what time period were second generation computers used?
   a. 1939–1944
   b. 1945–1957
   c. 1958–1964
   d. 1965–present

8. Which of the following are used in third generation computers?
   a. integrated circuits
   b. transistors
   c. vacuum tubes
   d. gears and levers

9. How long had we been using second generation computers when third generation computers came into use?
   a. 5 years
   b. 12 years
   c. 6 years
   d. 20 years

10. Which of the following is *not* likely to happen in the near future?
    a. computers will become smaller
    b. computers will be faster
    c. computers will be more reliable
    d. computers will be obsolete

Skill Enhancement

Review of the Tense System in English

There are twelve active tenses in English. Using verb tenses correctly shows a true understanding of the language. Verb tenses show the time relationships between actions or events almost as clearly as dates and times do. Understanding these relationships will help you better understand everything you read.

1. The *simple present* indicates an habitual or repeated action or a state in the present:

Example: People depend on computers with integrated circuits every day throughout the world.

The simple present can also be used as the historical present and is used to express universal statements.

Example: Dr. John von Neumann developed what we refer to as the stored program concept.

A time line depicting the simple present tense might look like this. Each vertical line refers to the repetition of the action in the present.

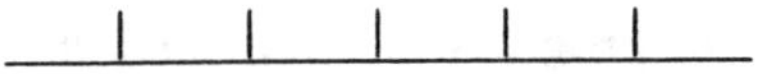

2. The *present progressive** or *present continuous* indicates an action that is happening, that is in progress, right now or at a present moment.

Example: Due to the fact that scientists are constantly making advances in technology, it is likely that the pattern of past developments will continue.

A time line depicting the present progressive might look like this:

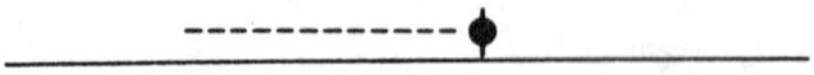

The vertical line here represents a moment in the present, either right now or at a repeated moment in the present. The circle around the vertical line shows that the action is in progress at the present moment.

3. The *present perfect* indicates an action which happened before the present moment, goes up to that moment and can occur again in the present or in the future. For example, we cannot say, "Gottfried Leibnitz has made advances in technology" because that action cannot happen again. The present perfect always shows a relationship between the action and a present moment, but does *not* indicate that the action is in progress at the present moment. If the present moment is not stated, we understand it to be now.

Example: In fact, these unequalled developments in computer technology have occurred only since the end of the war. (They can continue to occur.)

A time line representing the present perfect might look like this:

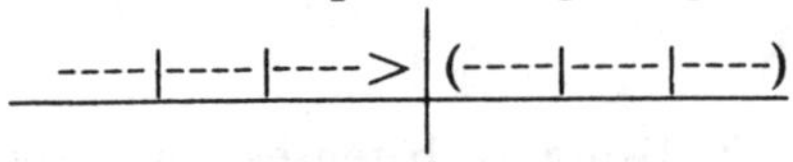

(present moment)

The arrow indicates that the action happened before the present moment. The line in parentheses after the present moment indicates that the action *can* happen again.

4. The *present perfect progressive** or *present perfect continuous* is like the present perfect in that it shows a relationship between an action and a present moment. However, the action is *in progress* at the present moment. We know this because the *duration* of the action—how long the action has been happening—is clearly stated. Therefore, there are *two* conditions for the present perfect progressive: 1. present moment 2. statement of duration.

Example: Computer companies have been using integrated circuits in computers ever since 1965.

In this statement, we understand that the present moment is now. The duration is indicated in the phrase "ever since 1965."

A time line representing the present perfect progressive might look like this:

(present moment)

The circle around the vertical line shows that the action is in progress at the present moment.

5. The *simple past* indicates a completed action in the past, even if we know the total duration of that action.

Example: He began to work on the EDSAC (*E*lectronic *D*elay *S*torage *A*utomatic *C*alculator) and completed it in 1949.

A time line depicting the simple past might look like this:

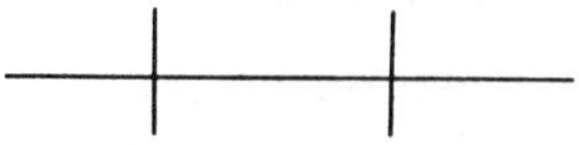

or like this:

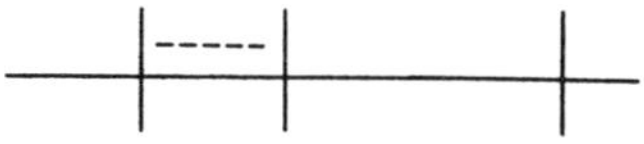

6. The *past progressive* or *past continuous* indicates an incomplete action in the past. When it is used with the simple past, the verb in the simple past interrupts the action of the past progressive.

Example: While they were working on the EDVAC, Mauchly and Eckert formed their own computer company.

When the past progressive is used with another past progressive, the actions are simultaneous (they occur at the same time).

Example: While von Neumann was working with Eckert and Mauchly at the University of Pennsylvania, Maurice V. Wilkes was attending classes there.

A time line depicting the past progressive might look like this:

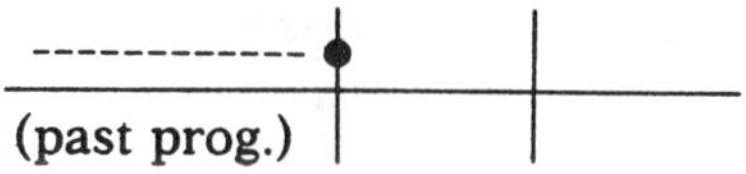

or like this:

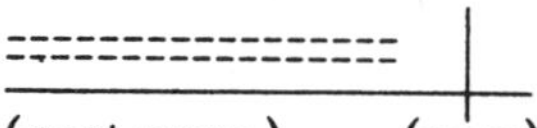

7. The *past perfect* indicates an action that began before a *past* moment and extended to that moment or happened repeatedly before that moment.

Example: By 1956, IBM had become the largest U.S. computer company.

A time line depicting the past perfect might look like this:

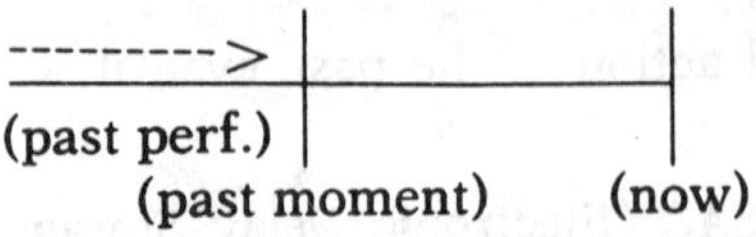

8. The _past perfect progressive_* or *past perfect continuous* indicates an action that continued up to the past moment. As in the case of the present perfect progressive, we have two conditions: 1. past moment 2. duration.

Example: They had been working for three years when they completed the programming language FORTRAN (*FOR*mula *TRAN*slation).

A time line depicting the present perfect progressive might look like this:

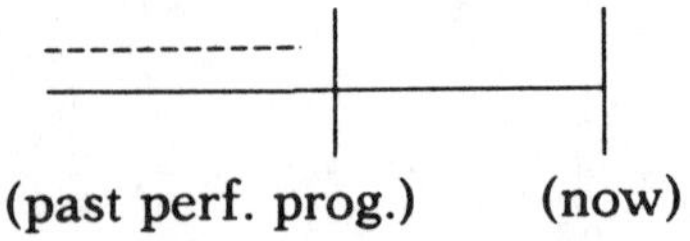

9. The *simple future* indicates a simple or repeated action that will occur after the present moment. Both "will" and "going to" can express the future. Sometimes the simple present or present progressive indicates future.

Example: Due to the fact that scientists are constantly making advances in technology, it is likely that the pattern of past developments will continue.

A time line depicting the simple future tense might look like this:

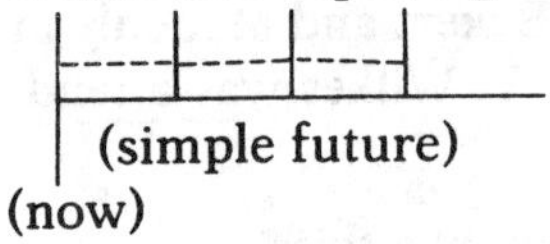

10. The _future progressive_* indicates an action that is *in progress* at a future moment.

Example: That is, in the future, we will probably be using computers that are smaller, faster, cheaper, more powerful, and more reliable than the ones we are using right now.

A time line depicting the future progressive might look like this:

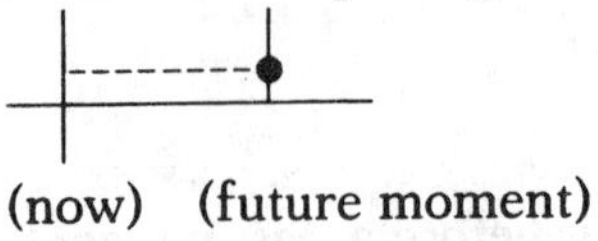

11. The *future perfect* indicates an action that will begin before a future moment and will extend to that moment or will happen repeatedly before that moment.

Example: It is probable that, by the year 2000, computer technology will have advanced so much that today's computers will be completely outdated—they will be obsolete.

A time line depicting the future perfect might look like this:

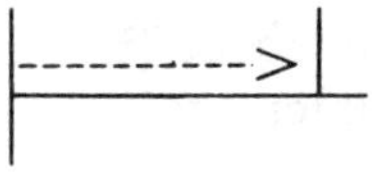

(now) (future moment)

12. The *future perfect progressive* or *future perfect continuous* indicates an action that will begin before a future moment and will be *in progress* at that moment. We also know the duration of the action. The two conditions for future perfect progressive are: 1. future moment and 2. stated duration.

Example: Although people will have been relying on computers for only about 55 years or so by that time, it will probably be very difficult to imagine life without these devices.

A time line depicting the future perfect progressive might look like this:

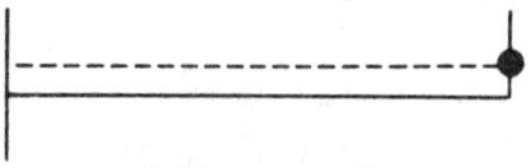

(duration)
(now) (future moment)

A. Complete the following sentences from the reading with the correct tense and form of the verb in parentheses. Refer to the reading only if necessary.

1. Near the end of World War II, Dr. John von Neumann developed what we _____ (refer) to as the stored program concept.
2. Designers _____ (use) the stored program concept in building digital computers ever since von Neumann first explained his theory.
3. While von Neumann _____ (work) with Eckert and Mauchly at the University of Pennsylvania, Maurice V. Wilkes _________ (attend) classes there.
4. When Wilkes _____ (return) to Cambridge University in England, he _____ (bring) the idea of the stored program with him.
5. The EDSAC, the first stored program computer, _____ (work) for approximately two years when Mauchly and Eckert finished their stored program computer, the EDVAC (*E*lectronic *D*iscrete *V*ariable *A*utomatic *C*omputer) in 1951.
6. By the time all the votes were counted, UNIVAC's operators _____ (know) the probable results for many hours.
7. In 1952, Dr. Grace Hopper _____ (develop) the first of these programs.

8. By 1959, programmers ____ (invent) more than 200 programming languages.
9. It is probable that, by the year 2000, computer technology ____ (advance) so much that today's computers will be completely outdated—they will be obsolete.
10. Although people ____ (rely) on computers for only about 55 years or so by that time, it will probably be very difficult to imagine life without these devices.

B. Read the following paragraph carefully. Try to get an idea of the time relationships. Look for general time indicators (*in the past, now, in the future,* etc.). Fill in the blanks with the correct form and tense of the verb in parentheses.

The most significant advances in computer technology ____(take place) in the United States. In fact, the U.S. ____ (lead) the world in this area for many years. However, not long ago, the Japanese ____ (develop) the two fastest computers in the world. They ____ (work) on this machine for many years when they ____(announce) the news at the beginning of 1984.

Many computer companies in the United States ____ (be) concerned about losing business. However, people at Cray Research, Inc., one of the most important manufacturers of large computers in the U.S., say that they ____ (develop) new computers right now and that these computers ____ (be) ready for sale in the near future.

When the new Cray computers come out, people ____ (use) the Japanese computers for some time. Although technology ____ (advance) by then, no one is sure whether the new Cray computers ____ (be) faster than the Japanese computers.

Enrichment Activities

1. Explain the pattern of evolution that the development of the computer has followed. Show how computers have improved from generation to generation.
2. Make a time line depicting the evolution of computers that you have studied in this chapter and the previous one. Clearly show the time relationship between each development. Write sentences showing this relationship through the use of verb tenses.
3. Make predictions about the computer of the future. Discuss its size, cost, reliability, storage space, programming methods, etc.

*Remember that the progressive tenses can only be used with dynamic or action verbs. Stative verbs (be, belong, have, know, like, need, own, want, etc.) do not occur in the progressive.

6-4 Internal circuitry of an IBM disk drive.

CHAPTER 7

THE COMPUTER SYSTEM: PART I

The computer itself is just one component of what is generally referred to 1
as the computer system. All computer systems, whether personal computers or mainframes, have several parts. There are usually different devices which together make up the computer system. None of these devices is capable of functioning alone in a meaningful way. For example, complicated mathematical calculations performed by a computer would be meaningless if the results could not be communicated to a human user. Similarly, the computer could not even begin to perform those calculations if the human user had no way of telling the computer which numbers to use.

COMPUTER SYSTEM COMPONENTS

Any computer system consists of three main areas. As mentioned in Chap- 2
ter 1, all of data processing is divided into the three areas of input, processing, and output. The computer system is divided into these three areas as well (see illustration 1.4). The first component, or part, of the computer system is the area of input. This area would encompass any machine which is used to send data to the computer to be processed. It also includes any device that is used to store data and programs to be sent to the computer for processing. The second area consists of the CPU or central processing unit. This is where the actual work of the computer takes place. The third component of the computer system is that of output. This area includes any device that is used to transmit processed data, or information, from the CPU to an output form that can be understood by a human user. In this chapter the various devices used in the input and output areas

7-1 The computer itself is just one component of what is generally referred to as the computer system.

of the computer system will be discussed in detail. The following chapter
will deal with the CPU itself and various methods of data and information
storage within the computer system.

Machines that are used to either input data or output information are 3
referred to as *I/O* (input/output) *devices*. Some machines can be used for
both input and output. Others, however, are used only as either an input
device or an output device. Any device, whether input or output, that is
used in conjunction with the computer is referred to as a *peripheral* device.
That is, it works side by side with the computer. A peripheral device that
is connected directly to the computer by cables or wires is called an *on-line peripheral* device. Those machines which are used in the computer
system, but are not connected directly to the CPU itself, are called *off-line
peripheral* devices. Most of the machines now used in computer systems
are on-line devices.

INPUT DEVICES

Input devices, the machines that make up the first area of the computer 4
system, are on-line peripheral devices that are used to transmit data to the
CPU. If we wanted to add a series of numbers using the computer, the
numbers to be added would be transmitted to the CPU by one of the fol-
lowing devices. The *computer terminal* (see illustration 7.1) is, perhaps, the
most common input device in the computer system. (It is also used as an
output device.) The terminal usually consists of a keyboard (which looks
like a typewriter) and a screen called a CRT (*C*athode *R*ay *T*ube). Most
microcomputer systems use a keyboard to input data. Data are entered by
means of the keyboard and transmitted to the CPU. The CRT screen allows
the user to view the data being entered. A terminal that uses a screen is
also referred to as a VDT (*V*ideo *D*isplay *T*erminal).

If punched cards (see Chapter 10) are used as input in a particular 5
computer system, then an input device known as a *card reader* is needed.
The card reader "reads" the data in the punched holes by using wire
brushes or light beams. It then converts, or changes, this data into elec-
tronic signals or pulses which can be understood by the computer.

The *console* is a computer terminal that has special functions. The 6
computer operator, whose job is to keep the system running smoothly,
uses this machine for several purposes. He or she can control the other
machines in the system and can enter input by means of the console. The
operator can also use the console to communicate with other users by
sending messages from the console to the individual terminals in the
system.

Another input device that is used in some systems is called a *M*agnetic 7
*I*nk *C*haracter *R*eader (MICR). This machine "reads" characters made
with a magnetized ink and transmits the data to the CPU. Characters made
with magnetic ink are readable by both humans and machines. A bank,
for example, would use a MICR to input the account number on the bot-
tom of a personal check.

An input device that is used more and more frequently is the *optical* 8
scanner or the *optical mark recognition* device. It is referred to as "optical" because it works in a way that is not dissimilar to the way the human eye works. Such a machine "reads" coded symbols and transmits them as electrical signals to the CPU. Many standardized tests, like the TOEFL, are scored, that is, graded, by a computer. The data from these tests are entered by means of an optical mark recognition device. Many supermarkets use optical scanners to "read" the data from the *U*niversal *P*roduct *C*ode (UPC) (see illustration 7.2) in order to determine prices and keep current inventories.

A *magnetic tape drive* is used to convert data stored on magnetic tape 9
into electrical signals which can be understood by the CPU. As such, it functions as an input device. It can also be an output device when it is used to record output from the CPU on magnetic tape. The function of a *magnetic disk drive* is similar to that of a tape drive. The disk drive, however, is used with magnetic disk storage. While the disk drive used in a large computer system is a fairly large machine, that used with the typical microcomputer is often a small box-shaped device (see illustration 7.3). Both magnetic tape and magnetic disk storage will be discussed in the following chapter.

Other sophisticated input devices will become quite common in the 10
near future. *Voice input* devices, for example, which are also called *speech recognition* devices, will be a very popular input method. Handicapped people will be able to communicate with the CPU in some systems by means of eye movements. Although such input devices are very advanced, they will be seen often in computer systems over the next few years.

7-2 Supermarkets use optical scanners to "read" the data from the Universal Product Code (shown right) in order to record prices and keep current inventories.

7-3 Disk drive used with an Apple microcomputer.

OUTPUT DEVICES

There are several types of output devices. Some of them, such as tape and disk drives and terminals, are also used as input devices. When a terminal or video monitor is used as an output device, the information it displays on the screen is called *soft copy*. This means that the information shown is temporary. Another kind of output device is needed to obtain a permanent copy of the information. 11

The device used to get a printed, permanent copy, or *hard copy*, of information is called a *printer*. Printers are divided into two major types: *impact* and *nonimpact*. When an impact printer receives signals from the CPU, the characters in the printer strike the paper in much the same way as those in a typewriter hit the paper. Some of these printers print only 12

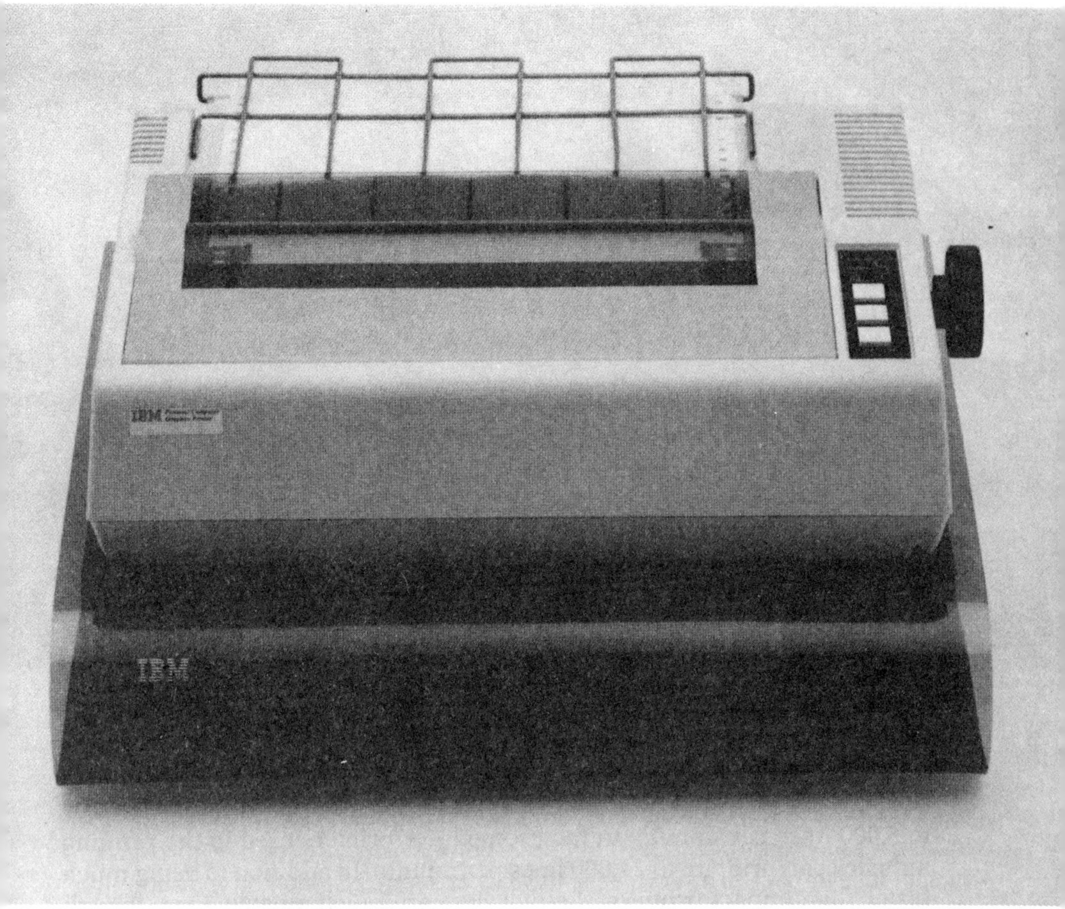

7-4 A printer provides a permanent, or hard, copy of computer-generated information.

one character at a time, although they can print approximately 900 characters a minute. Other impact printers, called line printers, print one line at a time. The fastest of these printers can print about 2,000 lines per minute (see illustration 7.4).

There are two basic printing methods used by impact printers. *Dot-* 13
matrix printers form letters, numbers, and symbols by means of tiny hammers which strike the paper. Each hammer produces a dot or point on the paper and the way these dots are arranged forms the letter. *Letter-quality* impact printers use a wheel or cup that contains each letter, number, and symbol. These printers are a slower and more expensive method of output than dot-matrix printers; however, their print quality is much better.

Nonimpact printers are newer than impact printers. These printers 14
operate by means of heat and heat-sensitive paper, electrical charges (positive and negative), or laser beams. Some nonimpact printers can print up

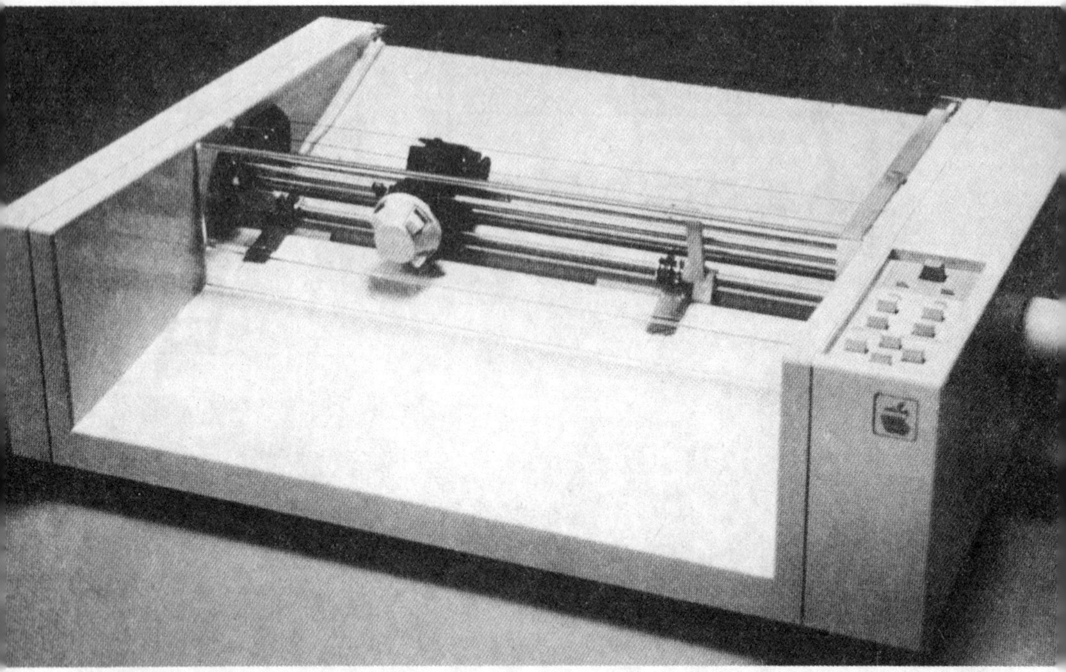

7-5 A plotter is a special device that is used to display output in graphic, or picture, form.

to 5,000 lines per minute. In fact, some laser printers used in the printing industry can print up to 21,000 lines per minute. In addition to being much faster than impact printers, these devices are much quieter. Even though they are more expensive than impact printers, they will probably replace impact printers in the years to come because they can print special characters and can be used with special forms.

A *plotter* is a special kind of device that, like impact and nonimpact 15
printers, also produces hard copy. It is used to display output in graphic, or picture, form. Instead of actually printing the output, the plotter draws it. One type of plotter has a long arm and a needle-like point which draws the output. This device is useful in making graphs and charts (see illustration 7.5).

The output device used in conjunction with punched cards (see Chap- 16
ter 10) is called a *card punch.* This machine receives signals from the CPU and converts these signals into the Hollerith Code. The coded information is then punched onto cards. Sometimes the card punch and the card reader are part of the same I/O device. The card punch is only useful in a computer system that uses punched cards as a form of input and output. However, these systems are no longer very common.

There are other devices in the computer system that are used with 17
these input and output devices. These devices help both the input and out-

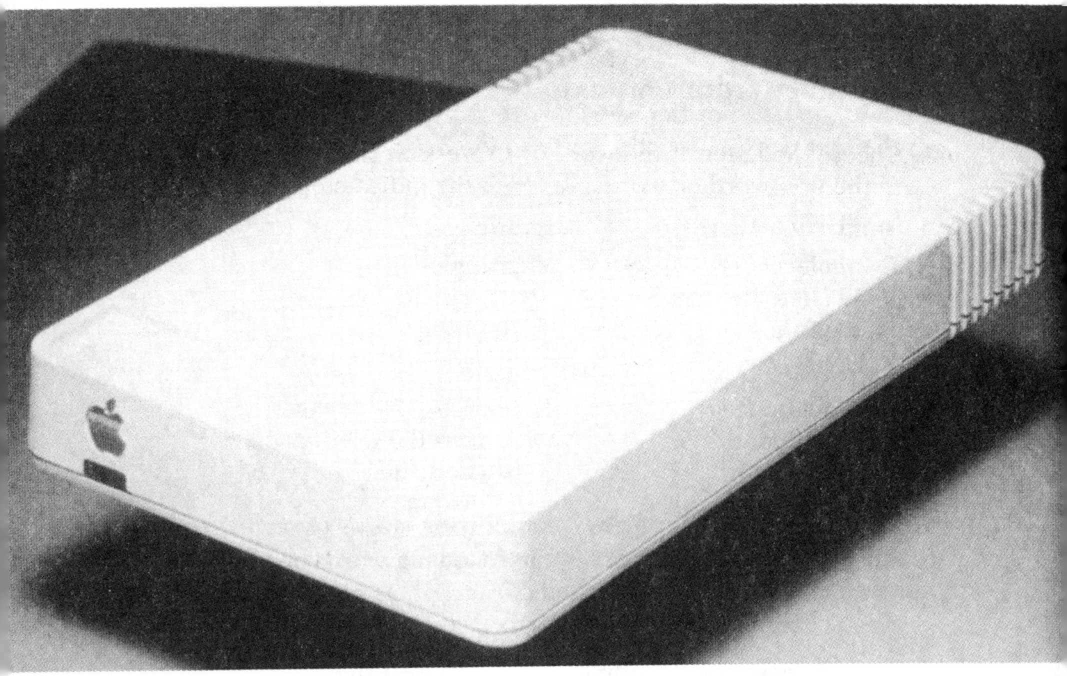

7-6 The modem is used to connect remote, or distant, terminals to the CPU.

put to arrive at the proper destination (either the CPU or an output device). The first of these devices is a *modem*. The modem is used to connect remote, or distant, terminals to the CPU. In one type of modem, the telephone receiver is placed into the device (see illustration 7.6) and the electronic signals are sent over the telephone. Modem stands for *MOD*ulation-*DEM*odulation, which refers to the way the device changes electrical signals from the computer into wave patterns that travel over telephone lines in the same way that the human voice travels over these lines. A modem is needed at both locations: one at the distant terminal or other I/O device, and the other at the CPU.

Machines called *multiplexors* and *concentrators* are used to increase 18
the number of terminals that can be used in a large computer system. Both devices receive input from many terminals and then transmit the data at a high speed to the computer system. Concentrators, however, are usually "smart" I/O devices. This means that they contain a microprocessor (a microchip) and can therefore be programmed. This increases the efficiency of the computer system.

The actual processing of data, of course, takes place in the CPU. In 19
the following chapter, we will study the CPU in detail. Methods of data storage outside the CPU will also be discussed.

EXERCISES

Vocabulary from Context

A. Choose the letter of the word or expression that is closest in meaning to the first word or words. Refer to the indicated paragraph as necessary.

1. similarly (1)
   a. alike
   b. in the same way
   c. likely
2. to obtain (11)
   a. to display
   b. to get
   c. to print
3. graphic (15)
   a. printed
   b. picture
   c. plotting
4. remote (17)
   a. over the telephone
   b. connected
   c. distant

B. Fill in the blanks with one of the following words or terms from the reading. Refer to the indicated paragraph as necessary. Be sure to use the correct grammatical form.

to encompass (2)	on-line (3)	off-line (3)
pulses (5)	to score (8)	to display (11)
to strike (12)		

1. It is not a good idea ____ a computer terminal. Hitting it will not make it function faster.
2. The keypunch is an ____ peripheral device. It isn't connected to the CPU.
3. ____ are electronic signals.
4. Many new devices were shown at the data processing exhibition, but the machines which ____ were very expensive.
5. An ____ peripheral device is connected directly to the computer.
6. The output component of the computer system ____ a number of devices. Among the machines it includes are the printer and the terminal.
7. In the past, teachers usually graded tests. Now computers can also ____ them.

C. Find each of the following words or terms in the indicated paragraph in the reading. Then write a synonym, definition, or description of the word or term.

1. CPU (2)
2. I/O devices (3)
3. computer terminal (4)
4. CRT (4)
5. VDT (4)
6. card reader (5)
7. console (6)
8. MICR (7)
9. UPC (8)
10. card punch (16)

Word Study—Stems and Affixes

There are several methods of trying to understand an unknown word without looking it up in the dictionary. The first way, understanding vocabulary from context, was discussed in Chapter 1, and you have been practicing it in every chapter until now. Understanding the meanings of the parts of the word can also help you guess the meaning of the word. Since many English words come from Greek and Latin, learning some Greek and Latin roots, or original words, can help us learn the meaning of the English words that they form a part of.

The main part of the word is called a stem. The parts that are added onto the beginning or end of the stem are called affixes. If the affix is added onto the beginning, it is called a prefix; if it is added onto the end, it is called a suffix. A prefix usually modifies, or changes, the meaning of a word. A suffix usually changes the part of speech.

7-7 Machines called multiplexors and concentrators are used to increase the number of terminals that can be used in a large computer system.

For example, "fix" is a stem which means to put or fix; "pre" is a prefix which means before. The word "prefix," therefore, refers to something that is put *before* a word.

Study the following stems and affixes.

Prefix	**Meaning**
com-, con-	together, with
dis-	not
il-, in-	not
mal-	bad, badly
mis-	wrong, wrongly
multi-	many
non-	not
peri-	around
re-	back, again
trans-	across

Stem	**Meaning**
-centr-	center
-graph-	writing
-junc-	join
-mit- (-miss-)	send
-opti-	of the eye
-phon-	sound
-pon-	put
-simil-	same, alike
-tele-	far, distant
-tempor-	time

Suffix	**Meaning—Part of Speech**
-able, -ible	capable of being—adj.
-ant, -ent	one in a specific state of condition—n. relating to a state or condition—adj.
-ate	to make—v.
-er, -or	the one who, the one that—n.
-ic, -ical	relating to—adj.
-tion, -ation	the act of—n.

A. Choose the correct meaning of the following words by analyzing the stems and affixes. If necessary, refer to the indicated paragraph in the reading and try to understand the word from context.

1. communicate (1)
   a. to make known
   b. to commune
   c. to output

2. to transmit (2)
   a. to input
   b. to output
   c. to send

3. peripheral (3)
   a. relating to a machine
   b. relating to the CPU
   c. relating to something around or near something else

4. video (4)
   a. relating to sound
   b. relating to vision
   c. relating to processing

5. to convert (5)
   a. to turn something into
   b. to read
   c. to input signals

6. optical (8)
   a. relating to lasers
   b. relating to vision
   c. relating to reading

7. dissimilar (8)
   a. not unlike
   b. not the same
   c. alike

8. temporary (11)
   a. permanent
   b. on time
   c. for a limited time

9. graphic (15)
   a. relating to graphs
   b. relating to writing
   c. relating to printers

B. Using word analysis, try to give a definition of each of the following words. Indicate the part of speech of each word.

1. component (1)
2. conjunction (3)
3. operator (6)
4. readable (7)
5. nonimpact (12)
6. telephone (17)
7. multiplexors (18)
8. concentrators (18)

Comprehension Exercises

A. True-False. Write "T" if the statement is true. Write "F" if it is false.

1. The CPU is just another term for the computer system.
2. None of the devices in the computer system can function alone in a meaningful way.
3. Most peripheral devices are off-line.
4. Output units transmit data to the CPU.
5. The console is *not* an ordinary terminal.
6. Banks make extensive use of magnetic ink character readers.
7. Optical mark recognition devices can see.
8. Standardized tests can be scored by computer.
9. Some machines can function as both input and output devices.
10. A printer produces soft copy.

B. Choose the letter of the *best* answer for each of the following.

1. Which of the following is *not* a component of the computer system?
   a. input
   b. output
   c. research
   d. processing

2. Which of the following could be either an input or output device?
   a. terminal
   b. card reader
   c. card punch
   d. printer

3. Which of the following is *not* a function of the console?
   a. input data
   b. control other devices in the computer system
   c. print hard copy
   d. communicate with other terminals

4. Which of the following would an optical mark recognition device be used for?
   a. reading punched cards
   b. reading product codes
   c. reading magnetic tape
   d. reading electronic signals

5. Which device produces hard copy?
   a. terminal
   b. card punch
   c. tape drive
   d. printer

6. Line printers ____.
   a. can print 21,000 lines per minute
   b. are faster than laser printers
   c. print one line at a time
   d. print one character at a time

7. Which of the following is *not* true of nonimpact printers?
   a. they are less costly than impact printers
   b. they will probably replace impact printers
   c. they are faster than impact printers
   d. they are quieter than impact printers

8. A plotter is ____.
   a. an input device
   b. used to produce printed output
   c. used to produce graphic output
   d. used to produce soft copy

9. A card punch ____.
   a. is an off-line peripheral device
   b. punches coded output onto punched cards
   c. transmits punched data to the CPU
   d. is the same as a card reader

10. A modem ____.
    a. connects long-distance telephones
    b. is part of the telephone
    c. connects remote terminals to the CPU
    d. increases the number of terminals

Skill Enhancement

Skimming

Skimming is an important reading skill that every English student should try to develop. Skimming involves reading a selection, or even a paragraph, quickly in order to get a general idea of the content. We usually skim a newspaper before choosing which articles to read in detail. Very often, we skim a reading or paragraph in order to determine the main idea.

In skimming a reading, we generally read titles and headings first. Then we look for important words which give clues to the general idea of the passage. We call these words *key words*. Sometimes these words are set off by punctuation (parentheses, quotation marks, apostrophes, commas, etc.), by capital letters, or by a different type of printing. Words or phrases that are repeated several times in a paragraph or reading give a clue concerning the subject or topic of that paragraph or reading. However, when we skim a paragraph or a reading, we try not to focus on one idea or one vocabulary item in particular, but rather to understand the author's main idea.

If we skim the first paragraph of this reading, for example, we can immediately see that the topic or subject of the paragraph is the computer system. After skimming the first paragraph, try to identify the main idea.

The main idea of the first paragraph is ____.

a. Computers can perform meaningful calculations.
b. The computer system consists of several devices or components.
c. None of the devices can function alone.
d. The human user tells the computer which figures to work with.

The correct answer is "b." As stated above, the computer system is the subject or topic of the paragraph.

A. In the following exercise, skim the paragraphs and then answer the questions.

Transmitting data by means of tiny beams of light—lasers—is becoming more and more popular in the computer industry. Lasers can flash approximately 90 million times per second. Each of these flashes represents a bit of information. Lasers, therefore, represent a very high-speed method of input and output.

1. What is the subject of the paragraph?
   a. input
   b. output
   c. data transmission
   d. lasers

2. What is the main idea of the paragraph?
   a. Lasers are tiny beams of light.
   b. Lasers can flash.
   c. Lasers can provide high-speed input and output.
   d. Flashes contain information.

Instead of transmitting data and information over wires, lasers transmit them over a very thin thread of glass called an *optical fiber.* These optical fibers are approximately as thin as a human hair. Even though lasers travel over these fibers at the speed of light (186,000 miles per second), they remain powerful over very long distances. Optical fibers are not only useful for transmitting signals for data processing purposes. They are also used in the communications field for the transmission of television shows and telephone conversations.

1. What is the subject of the paragraph?
   a. lasers
   b. optical fibers
   c. human hair
   d. data transmission

2. State the main idea of the paragraph in a complete sentence.

Data and information can be transmitted over long distances by means of a communications satellite which orbits, that is, revolves around, the earth. Such a satellite receives signals from one place on the earth and reflects these signals back to another place on earth. Satellite systems such as INTELSAT (*IN*ternational *TEL*ecommunications *SAT*ellite Consortium) and COMSAT (*COM*munications *SAT*ellite Corporation) place satellites in space to handle data, voice, and video transmissions.

1. Are there any key words in the paragraph? What are they?
2. What is the subject of the paragraph?
3. What is the main idea of the paragraph?

Enrichment Activities

1. Visit an establishment (supermarket, department store, etc.) that uses an optical scanner or an optical mark recognition device as a method of input. Give an oral report to your classmates describing the specifics of the use of that machine as an input device in the establishment you visited.

2. In the library, locate a publication dealing with computers (*Creative Computing*, *Personal Computing*, etc.). Choose one article from that publication. Skim each paragraph individually and write the main idea of each paragraph. Then skim the entire article and write the main idea of the article.

CHAPTER

8

THE COMPUTER SYSTEM: PART II

THE CPU

The CPU, or central processing unit, is often referred to as the heart of the 1
computer system. All of the computer functions studied in the first chapter take place in the CPU. The CPU has three main parts: the control unit, the arithmetic-logic unit, and the primary storage unit. Each of these areas has a specific function in the processing of data (illustration 8.1).

The *control unit* is like the "brain" of the computer system. This is 2
because this unit supervises and controls everything that takes place in the CPU. This part of the CPU determines the sequence or order of specific operations. For example, it is the control unit's job to make sure that multiplication is performed before addition. The control unit also acts as an interpreter because it translates the commands in a program and sends signals to the circuits to follow those instructions. Another function of the control unit is to direct the movement of data and information from the input area of the CPU to the output area of the CPU.

The *arithmetic-logic unit* (ALU) is the area where most of the actual 3
processing is done. Mathematical calculations are performed here. *Registers* or *accumulators* are special areas of the ALU that temporarily hold or store data. For example, in order to find an average, the computer must first add some numbers and then divide that total by the number of figures added. The intermediate result, in this case the total of the added numbers, is held in a register until the division takes place. The logical operations of the computer are also performed in the ALU. For example, the ALU can compare two numbers to determine which one is larger. It can also compare words to see if they are the same or different. Even though the ALU contains registers, it does not really store data. That is the *primary storage unit's* job.

The CPU, or central processing unit, is often referred to as the heart of the computer system.

THE CENTRAL PROCESSING UNIT

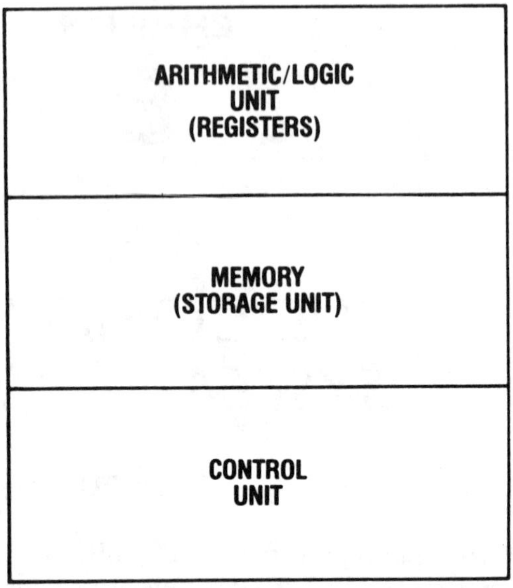

8-1

There are several different terms that refer to the primary storage 4
unit. Among these are internal (because it is inside the CPU) storage, main memory, and main storage. The primary storage unit holds the entire program, that is, all the data and the instructions for processing them. Although this unit holds all the instructions in a program, it is important to keep in mind that only one instruction can be carried out or completed at a time. Internal storage is like a group of boxes (see illustration 8.2). Only one instruction or one item of data can be stored in each box. As a piece of data is needed, the control unit takes it from the correct box. Each box has what we call an *address* so that the control unit can locate, or find, it. The control unit can go directly to the place in memory where a specific instruction or a specific item of data is located. Another way of referring to this direct access, or direct method of entry to the memory, is *random access*. For this reason, most modern computers, including microcomputers, are described as having *random access memory* (RAM). In some computers these addresses are actually tiny circles of metal with a hole in the center. These are called *cores* and they can be magnetized in a clockwise or counterclockwise direction. For this reason, internal storage is often called *core storage*. Newer CPUs have monolithic chips, sometimes called microchips. Memory that uses electronic components on an IC (Integrated Circuit) is called *semiconductor memory*. That part of computer memory which is built into the machine and can never be changed is called *read-only memory* (ROM).

AUXILIARY STORAGE

Although primary storage actually holds programs, it is not large enough 5
to store several programs at once. *Auxiliary storage*, also referred to as sec-

Internal Storage Main Memory

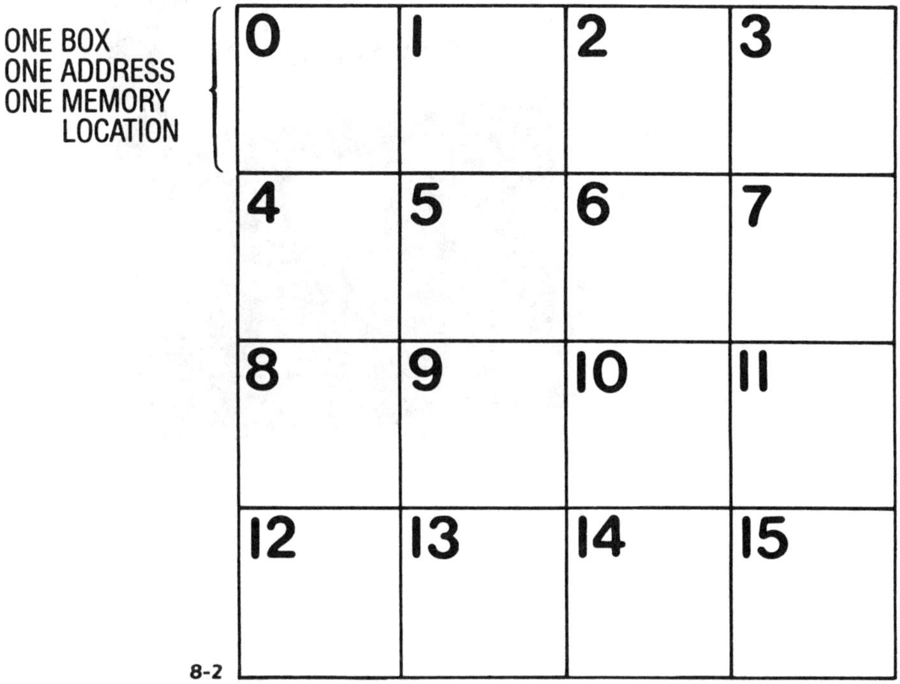

8-2

ondary storage, is needed. Auxiliary storage, which is really extra storage, is not actually located in the CPU, although it is connected to the CPU and controlled by it. There are several kinds of auxiliary storage: magnetic tape, magnetic disks, punched cards, paper tape, magnetic drums. Paper tape is similar to punched cards in that the data is stored in punched holes. Although paper tape can hold large amounts of data, it is still quite slow and easily torn. A magnetic drum is like a barrel whose surface is made of a material that can be magnetized. This outside coat contains data in the form of magnetized and unmagnetized spots. Neither of these forms of storage is common today.

MAGNETIC TAPE

The magnetic tape used for auxiliary storage is not dissimilar to that used 6
to record sound. The surface is made of a material that can be magnetized. The tape drive magnetizes areas on this surface in order to store data. Magnetic tape is generally ½″ (″ is the symbol used for inch) wide, but it can also come in widths of ¾″, 1″, or 3″. The device or container that mag-

8-3 A flexible disk, also called a floppy disk, is used primarily with microcomputers.

netic tape is kept on is called a *reel.* One reel is generally 10½″ in diameter (the distance across). The length of the tape can vary from 50′ to 2400′ or more (′ is the symbol used for feet). Records on magnetic tape are separated by blank spaces. These blank spaces are called *inter-record gaps* (IRGs). Cassette tape, which resembles the cassette tape used with small tape recorders, is used with some older microcomputers and in systems where a great deal of auxiliary storage is not required.

There are several advantages or benefits to using magnetic tape. One 7
of the pros is that magnetic tape can store vast amounts of data in a relatively small space. Therefore, it does not require a great amount of storage area. In addition, the length of each record on the tape is not limited to 80 characters, as it is on the punched card. Magnetic tape can also be erased and reused and is therefore economical.

There are also some disadvantages associated with using magnetic 8
tape. In order to locate a specific song on a sound tape, the user must start at the beginning of the tape. In the same way, in order to use a specific program or record on a magnetic tape, the tape must be run from the beginning. The access to the tape is called *sequential.* The order or sequence must be followed from beginning to end; the tape cannot start in the middle. This makes the magnetic tape a somewhat slow storage medium or method. Anyone who knows the Hollerith Code can read a punched card. The tape, however, is not readable by human users. Thus, the difficulty of correctly labeling the tape so it is accessible to a human user is another disadvantage.

MAGNETIC DISKS

A magnetic disk is similar to a phonograph record and is sometimes 9
referred to as a *hard disk* or, in the case of microcomputers, a *floppy disk*. The surface of the disk is made of a material that can be magnetized. There are approximately 200 concentric circles (one inside of the other) on a hard disk used in large computer systems. These circles are called *tracks* and data is stored in these tracks. Several hard disks may be used together in what is known as a *disk pack*. The disk drive rotates the entire disk pack so that all the disks turn at the same time. Disk drives can rotate at speeds anywhere from about 50 to about 1,000 revolutions per second. A flexible disk is unlike a hard disk because it is smaller and can be bent. This disk, which is also called a floppy disk or a diskette (see illustration 8.3), is used primarily with microcomputers. The floppy disk is usually

8-4 Access to programs stored on a disk is immediate or direct.

made of plastic and its cost is relatively low. Hard disks known as *Winchester disks* are also available for microcomputer systems. Although they hold much more information than floppy disks, they are quite expensive.

One of the advantages of using a disk as a storage device is that access 10
to programs on the disk is direct or immediate. For this reason, the disk is referred to as a *direct access storage device* (DASD). Just as a song in the middle of a phonograph record can be played immediately (without having to go through the previous songs), a program on a disk can be located immediately because a disk, like main memory, has addresses. For this reason, the disk is sometimes used as supplementary storage to main memory. Programs on disks are addressed by the number referring to the disk surface, if there is a disk pack, and the number of the track. Because access to the disk is direct, the disk is a much faster storage medium than the tape is. The magnetic disk, like the magnetic tape, can be revised, erased, and reused. The disk, however, greatly reduces the time required to access data (see illustration 8-4).

Among the disadvantages of the magnetic disk as a storage medium 11
is that many disks cannot store as much data as magnetic tape. In addition, the disk is fairly expensive. It can cost ten times as much as magnetic tape. Thus, with mainframes and minicomputers, a disk would not be used for applications where the amount and cost of storage are more important than the speed required to access the data. If, however, speed is an important factor in a particular system, the disk would be the preferred storage medium.

BACKUP STORAGE

Some computer systems make use of different types of storage media. For 12
example, the disk could be employed as the primary method of auxiliary storage because it provides immediate access. In such a case, the tape might be used as backup storage. That is, a copy of the disk would be made onto a tape at regular intervals (every day, every other day, every week, etc.). In this way, there would be a backup, that is, a copy, that could be used if something were accidentally erased from the disk. Magnetic tape is especially useful for this purpose. Microcomputer systems use additional diskettes or a hard disk for backup storage.

Magnetic disk and magnetic tape are the most common storage media 13
in use today. However, computer technology is constantly progressing. Laser devices are currently being developed as a storage medium. It is likely that such devices may ultimately replace all other storage media. No matter what the storage medium, it is important to remember that *all* components of the system work together for the single purpose of transforming data into information (see illustration 8.5).

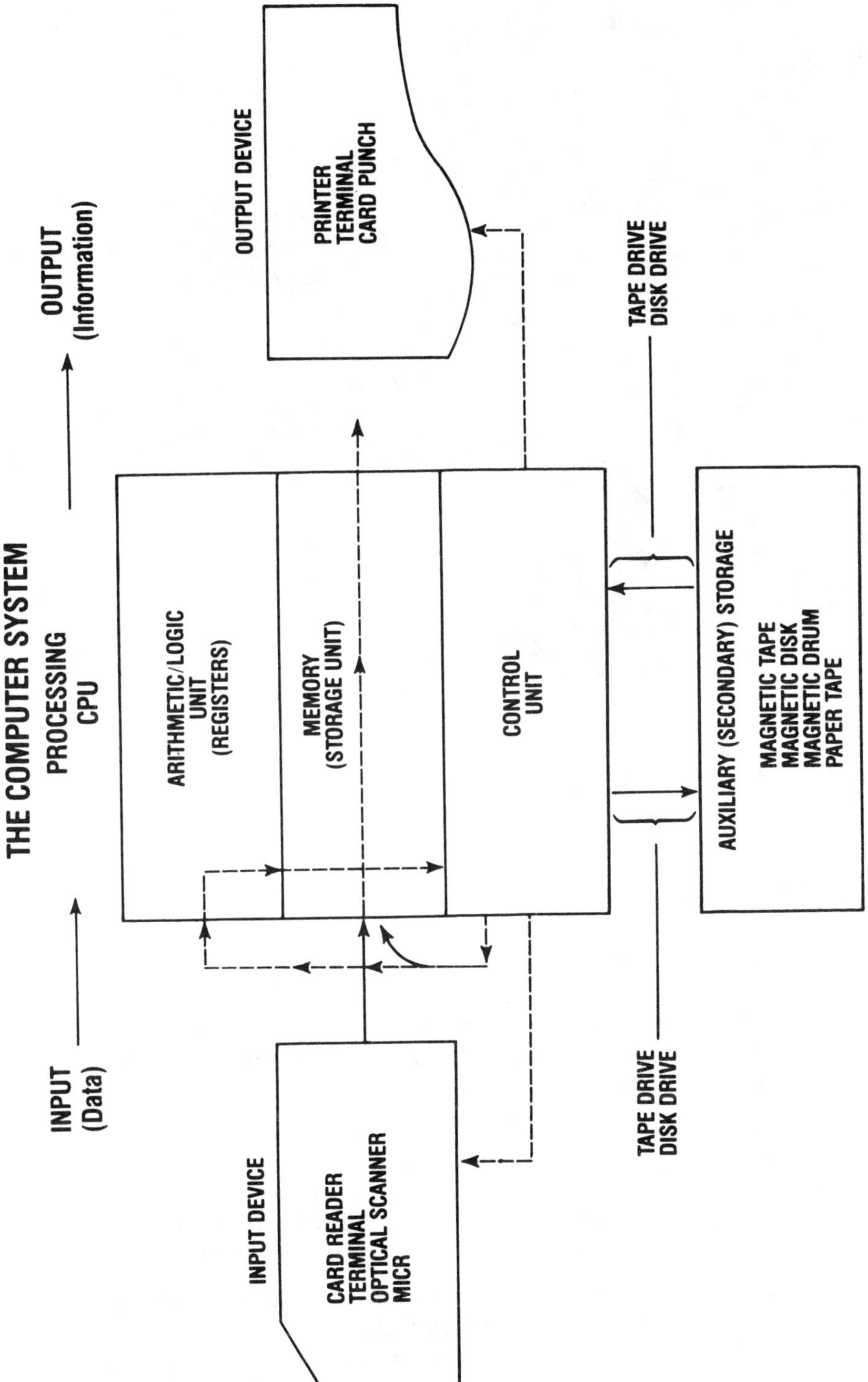
THE COMPUTER SYSTEM
INPUT
(Data)
PROCESSING
CPU
OUTPUT
(Information)
INPUT DEVICE
CARD READER
TERMINAL
OPTICAL SCANNER
MICR
ARITHMETIC/LOGIC
UNIT
(REGISTERS)
MEMORY
(STORAGE UNIT)
CONTROL
UNIT
OUTPUT DEVICE
PRINTER
TERMINAL
CARD PUNCH
TAPE DRIVE
DISK DRIVE
AUXILIARY (SECONDARY) STORAGE
MAGNETIC TAPE
MAGNETIC DISK
MAGNETIC DRUM
PAPER TAPE
TAPE DRIVE
DISK DRIVE

8-5 Back up storage is recommended to prevent loss of important data that could accidentally be erased.

EXERCISES

Vocabulary from Context

A. Fill in the blanks with one of the following words or terms from the reading. Refer to the indicated paragraph as necessary. Be sure to use the correct grammatical form.

to perform (3)	average (3)	to contain (3)
internal (4)	to keep in mind (4)	to carry out (4)
item (4)	surface (5)	to vary (6)
pro (7)	vast (7)	medium (8)
to rotate (9)	interval (12)	ultimately (13)

1. Although older magnetic devices turn at high speeds, the disk drive _____ the disk pack much faster.
2. A disk pack _____ several disks. The disks held in the pack are accessed directly.

3. The outer coating of the hard disk can be magnetized. The ____ of the floppy disk can also be magnetized.
4. Laser devices can store enormous amounts of data. Such ____ storage will make other devices obsolete.
5. One of the advantages of punched cards is their low cost. Another ____ is that they can be read by humans.
6. Regular periods of time are referred to as time ____ .
7. A disk is a form of external storage. ____ storage is inside the CPU.
8. There are several methods of storing data. Magnetic tape is one very popular storage ____ .
9. It is important ____ the disadvantages of each type of storage medium. We should also remember the advantages.
10. We obtain a student's ____ by adding his grades together and dividing by the number of grades he has.
11. Mathematical operations can be done by calculators. Computers are also used ____ these operations.
12. A computer always ____ instructions very carefully. If there is a problem in completing directions, there is probably a programming error.
13. One piece of data is referred to as an ____ of data.
14. The speed of the disk drive can go from 50 to 1,000 revolutions per second. The speed may ____ according to the quality of the disk drive.
15. It is likely that, in the end, today's storage devices will no longer be used. They will ____ be replaced by more efficient media.

B. Find each of the following words or terms in the indicated paragraph in the reading. Then write a synonym, definition, or description of the word or term.

1. control unit (2)
2. ALU (3)
3. registers (3)
4. address (4)
5. RAM (4)
6. core storage (4)
7. auxiliary storage (5)
8. magnetic drum (5)
9. reel (6)
10. cassette tape (6)
11. track (9)
12. disk pack (9)
13. floppy disk (9)
14. DASD (10)
15. backup storage (12)

Word Study—Stems and Affixes

Review the stems and affixes studied in the previous chapter. Then study the following new stems and affixes.

Prefix	**Meaning**
dia-	across
inter-	between
micro-	small
mono-	one
pre-	before
sup-	under
super-	above, over
un-	not

Stem	**Meaning**
-ced-, -cess-	go, yield
-duc-	lead
-flect-, -flex-,	bend
-loc-	place
-log-, -ology-	study, speech
-lith-	stone
-meter-, -metr-	measure
-sequ-, -secut-	follow
-volu-, -volve-	roll, turn

Suffix	**Meaning—Part of Speech**
-ance, -ence	condition, quality—n.
-ize	to make—v.
-ly	like—adv.

Word Study Exercises

A. Choose the correct meaning of the following words by analyzing the stems and affixes. If necessary, refer to the indicated paragraph in the reading and try to understand the word from context.

1. temporarily (3)
   a. for a short time
   b. forever
   c. always

2. intermediate (3)
   a. between the beginning and end
   b. final
   c. calculation

3. locate (4)
   a. correct
   b. control the data
   c. find the place

4. diameter (6)
   a. inches
   b. measurement around
   c. measurement across

5. inter-record gaps (6)
   a. spaces after records
   b. spaces between records
   c. spaces before records

6. benefit (7)
   a. devices
   b. drawback
   c. good reason or result

7. reused (7)
   a. used once
   b. used again
   c. used many times

8. sequence (8)
   a. operation
   b. condition of having one thing follow another
   c. many orders

9. readable (8)
   a. unintelligible
   b. capable of being read
   c. incapable of being read

10. previous (10)
    a. coming before
    b. coming after
    c. reappearing

11. likely (13)
    a. friendly
    b. probable
    c. certain

12. replace (13)
    a. take the place of
    b. put back
    c. return

B. Using word analysis, try to give a definition of each of the following words. Indicate the part of speech of each word.

1. supervise (2)
2. multiplication (2)
3. interpreter (2)
4. monolithic (4)
5. sequential (8)
6. accessible (8)
7. concentric (9)
8. revolutions (9)
9. flexible (9)
10. revised (10)
11. reduces (10)
12. technology (13)

Comprehension Exercises

A. True-False. Write a "T" if the statement is true. Write "F" if it is false.

1. The functions of each part of the CPU overlap.
2. The control unit performs multiplication.
3. Most processing takes place in the ALU.
4. Random access is direct access.
5. Auxiliary storage is extra storage.
6. A magnetic disk is a form of primary storage.
7. Magnetic tapes and disks are the most usual types of auxiliary storage.
8. Magnetic tape can come in various widths.
9. The access to magnetic tape is direct.
10. Laser devices will probably not be used very much as storage media in the future.

B. Choose the letter of the *best* answer for each of the following.

1. Which of the following is *not* a function of the control unit?
   a. to determine the sequence of operations
   b. to transmit signals to the disk
   c. to act as interpreter between the program and the circuits
   d. to direct movement from the input area to the output area of the CPU

2. Where are the accumulators, or registers, located?
   a. in the IRGs
   b. in the control unit
   c. in the ALU
   d. in main memory

3. Which of the following is *not* another term for main memory?
   a. address
   b. primary storage
   c. internal storage
   d. main storage

4. Which storage medium is used for secondary storage?
   a. vacuum tubes
   b. microchips
   c. magnetic disks
   d. magnetic cores
5. Which of the following is the most common form of auxiliary storage?
   a. punched cards
   b. paper tape
   c. magnetic drum
   d. magnetic tape
6. How are records on magnetic tape separated?
   a. by tracks
   b. by blank spaces
   c. by punched holes
   d. by magnetized spots

8-6 Many adults use microcomputers to supplement their children's education or to enrich their own knowledge.

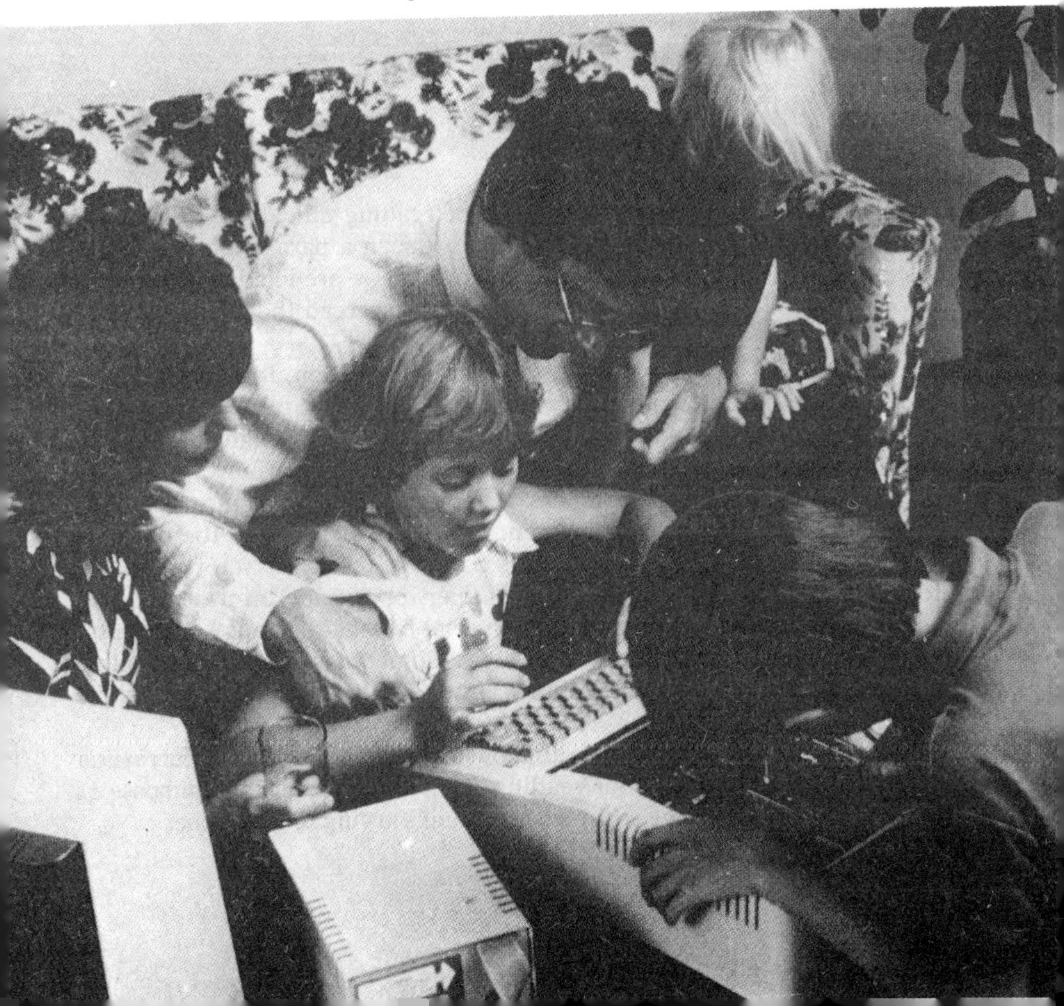

7. Which of the following is a disadvantage of magnetic tape?
   a. it holds large amounts of data
   b. it is inexpensive
   c. it has sequential access
   d. it requires little storage area

8. To what is a magnetic disk compared in the reading?
   a. to a record
   b. to a phonograph
   c. to a cassette
   d. to a microcomputer

9. Why is direct access preferable to sequential access?
   a. it is cheaper
   b. it is larger
   c. it is more important
   d. it is faster

10. Why is backup storage important?
    a. to prevent mistakes
    b. to prevent the permanent loss of files due to error
    c. to utilize magnetic tape
    d. to develop new storage media

Skill Enhancement

Scanning

Scanning, like skimming, is a method of reading quickly. However, the purpose of scanning is different. When we scan a paragraph or reading selection, instead of looking for the main idea, we are looking for specific information or details. For example, the way we read the telephone book is by scanning.

Before you begin to scan for specific information, it is important to decide what that information is and what form it will take. For example, in response to a question beginning with "when" you might decide that you are looking for a date. In that case you would move your eyes quickly over the page, looking for numbers. If you are looking for a measurement, you would probably also scan for numbers. In response to the question "who," you would look for a person's name. In that case, you would look for capital letters. When you are scanning for specific information, you should pay attention to punctuation. Special facts and details are often set apart by commas, dashes, or parentheses. Sometimes they follow a colon. A title, for example, would appear in quotation marks or would be underlined.

It is important to remember that once you have found the information you should not continue your reading. That would defeat the purpose of scanning, since when we scan, we are usually trying to save time.

A. Scan the reading in order to answer the following questions. Use the clues in parentheses to help you find the answer. Try not to spend more than three minutes on the entire exercise.

1. How many parts does the CPU contain? (Look for a number.)
2. What is the acronym for the place where most of the processing is done? (Look for capital letters.)
3. Why is primary storage also called internal storage? (Look for special punctuation marks.)
4. How long can magnetic tape be? (Look for numbers and special symbols.)
5. How fast can a disk drive rotate? (Look for numbers.)

B. Scan the reading in order to answer the following questions. Remember to decide what you are looking for before you begin scanning. Try not to spend more than five minutes on the entire exercise.

1. What is the acronym that refers to memory that is directly accessed?
2. What is the symbol used for feet?
3. What does diameter mean?
4. What is the most common width of magnetic tape?
5. What is the acronym that refers to the spaces between records on magnetic tape?
6. Approximately how many concentric circles are there on a magnetic disk?
7. What is the meaning of DASD?
8. Give some examples of time intervals from the reading.

Enrichment Activities

1. In small groups, design scanning exercises based on the chapters in this book or on the table of contents. Put a time limit on the exercises and give them to the other members of the class. Decide on some kind of reward for the individual who is able to complete each exercise in the least amount of time with the fewest errors.

2. Make a chart listing the pros and cons of magnetic tape versus magnetic disk as a storage medium. Suggest applications that would require the tape and those which would probably require the disk as the best method of storage.

AT&T
AT&T

CHAPTER

9

OVERVIEW OF COMPUTER TYPES: THE MICRO, THE MINI, AND THE MAINFRAME

Just 30 years ago, the term computer almost always referred to the large 1
and powerful computer which filled an entire room. Today, upon hearing the word computer, some people still think first of this large mainframe. Others, however, immediately think of the microcomputer, popularly called the personal computer, whose use is increasing daily. We will discuss the different kinds of computers in use today in this chapter.

TYPES OF COMPUTERS: DIGITAL AND ANALOG

There are two basic types of computers—the *digital* computer and the 2
analog computer. These two types of computers are very different; while the purpose of the digital computer is to count, the purpose of the analog computer is to measure. The digital computer counts by utilizing a series of digits to represent numbers. In contrast, the analog computer uses analogy to represent numbers; it represents numbers by measuring such things as electricity or temperature. The speedometer in a car works in much the same way as an analog computer works.

Compared to the analog computer, the digital computer is more accu- 3
rate and more versatile. Unlike the digital computer, which has a very large number of applications in a variety of fields such as business and government, the analog computer is used mainly for scientific applications in laboratory environments.

9-1 The average microcomputer is a self-contained device that has its own central processing unit.

TYPES OF DIGITAL COMPUTERS: SPECIAL PURPOSE AND GENERAL PURPOSE

There are two main types of digital computers—the special purpose and 4
the general purpose computer. As its name implies, the special purpose computer is designed for a single and unique purpose. Examples of special purpose computers are those in air traffic or military defense systems. In contrast, the general purpose computer, as its name also implies, can have a variety of applications in different areas. This is possible through the use of appropriate software. Just as a person is able to change clothes, a general purpose computer can change its "clothes," that is, its particular application, depending on the instructions it receives. Therefore, the same general purpose computer can be used for business, scientific, educational, or even entertainment purposes.

TYPES OF GENERAL PURPOSE COMPUTERS: MICROS, MINIS, MAINFRAMES

The differences between computer types are not limited to the contrast 5
between the analog and digital computers on the one hand, and the classification of digital computers into special purpose and general purpose machines on the other hand. General purpose computers are also divided into different types, depending upon the computer's power, speed, and size. There are three main types of general purpose computers—the small microcomputer, the medium-sized minicomputer, and the large mainframe. In spite of the fact that these computers are different, they all have the same basic components—a processor unit, input and output devices, and secondary or auxiliary storage units. All computers also carry out the same basic functions.

THE MICROCOMPUTER OR THE PERSONAL COMPUTER

The microcomputer, or personal computer, is the smallest of all general 6
purpose computers. The average "micro," or PC, as it is also called, is a self-contained unit, and has its own CPU and input and output devices (see illustration 9.1). The personal computer is designed to be used by only one person at a time. These computers are also "desk-top" computers and are able to fit on top of a desk or table. While personal computers may vary in size, most are fairly portable and can be carried from place to place. In fact, some personal computers, called briefcase computers, are so small and portable that they can be carried anywhere. The microcomputer is also designed to be "user friendly," that is, easily understood and operated by the average person. Although other languages are available for micros, BASIC is the most frequently used language for personal computers.

Micros are currently used for different purposes in many fields 7
including business, the home, and education, as discussed in Chapter 3. Because of this, the same computer might be used for performing complex business analyses, for word processing—the use of special programs in order to produce neat and accurate typed documents—or for playing games. To be more specific, in business, personal computers can do many things, including computing payrolls, predicting a company's future growth by carrying out complex analyses with financial planning programs, or producing colorful charts and graphs. In the home, micros can be used for such things as balancing checkbooks, typing letters, or playing games. Educational uses of micros include *computer-assisted instruction* (CAI), which helps students learn or practice information, and type homework. As we learned earlier, microcomputers can even help artists draw pictures, and musicians compose music.

INPUT DEVICES FOR MICROCOMPUTERS

The microcomputer system, like all other computer systems, consists of a 8
CPU, input/output devices, and auxiliary storage. However, because of the physical size of the microcomputer, some of these devices may be very different from those used with the larger computer systems. Input devices for the personal computer include several different things. The most common means of inputting data into a micro, like any other computer, is with a keyboard. The *computer keyboard* looks like the keyboard of a typewriter, but sends special signals to the CPU of the computer. Several other input devices are used very frequently with microcomputers. These devices, most of which are also available for use with mainframes, although used much less frequently, include joysticks, light pens, and touch screens (see illustration 9.2). *Joysticks* are very popular input devices and are used for playing computerized games. A *light pen*, like a joystick, is an input device attached to the computer. In fact, it looks like an ordinary pen. When aimed at the screen, however, it detects light and transmits it to the CPU of the computer. Unlike the keyboard, no typing is necessary when using a light pen. Light pens are especially helpful for drawing pictures with a computer. Another means of inputting information to the computer is the *touch screen*. The touch screen is sensitive to touch. It is very easy to use, as lightly touching the screen is all that is needed to give instructions to the computer. Another input device for micros is a *voice input device*. Voice input devices allow commands to be spoken directly to the computer. While voice devices are used today, they are not as common as the other input devices for micros. They are also very expensive. In the future, however, voice input might well replace the keyboard and be used to command robots as well.

OUTPUT DEVICES FOR MICROCOMPUTERS

The most commonly used output devices for microcomputers are video 9
monitors. Video monitors resemble television sets but receive the information to be displayed from the computer itself (see illustration 9.3). Television sets can also be connected to personal computers and used as video devices. Printers, both of the letter quality and dot-matrix type described earlier in the text, are also common output devices for personal computers.

AUXILIARY STORAGE FOR MICROCOMPUTERS

The auxiliary storage of a microcomputer is quite different from the aux- 10
iliary storage of larger computers. Personal computers generally store data on diskettes or floppy disks. These disks, which are made of a flexible material, come in several sizes. Disks of 8 inches (8″), 5 and ¼ inches (5¼″), and 3 and ½ inches (3½″) are the most common (see illustration 8.3). In order to access the information stored on the diskettes, the floppy disks are inserted into disk drives. These disk drives, like the rest of the micro itself, are usually quite small. Older microcomputers, unlike newer models, do not use floppy disks for auxiliary storage, but instead use cassette tapes. In addition, another type of auxiliary storage is available for personal computers. This is the hard disk of the type mentioned earlier in this text.

MICROCOMPUTER SYSTEMS

Currently, the most typical personal computer systems are composed of 11
the CPU, a keyboard, a video monitor and two disk drives. A printer is very often included in the typical microcomputer system. Although the components of the system may be the same, individual systems may be configured, that is, set up, in a number of ways. For example, the CPU, keyboard, monitor, and disk drives may make up one complete unit. In another system, the CPU and the keyboard may be together, with the monitor and the disk drives set up separately. In still another system the CPU and the disk drives may be combined into one component, with a separate monitor and a separate keyboard (see illustration 9.1).

MICROCOMPUTER GRAPHICS

Finally, the area of graphics, the computer's method of representing 12
objects, is important to our discussion (see illustration 9.3). Microcomputers differ significantly from other types of computers in regard to graph-

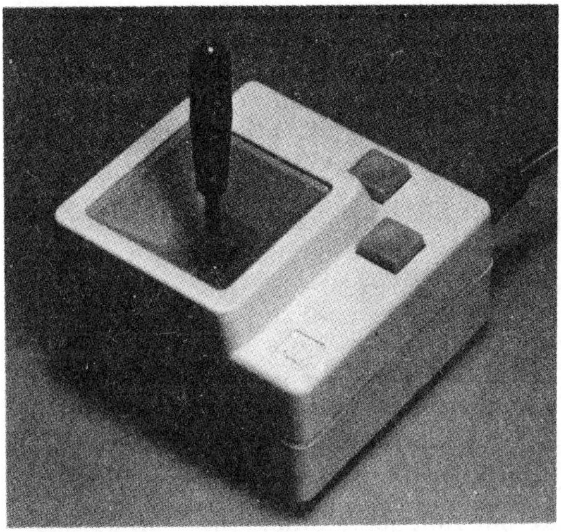

9-2 Joysticks are popular input devices that are used for playing computerized games.

9-3 Video monitors receive the information to be displayed from the computer itself.

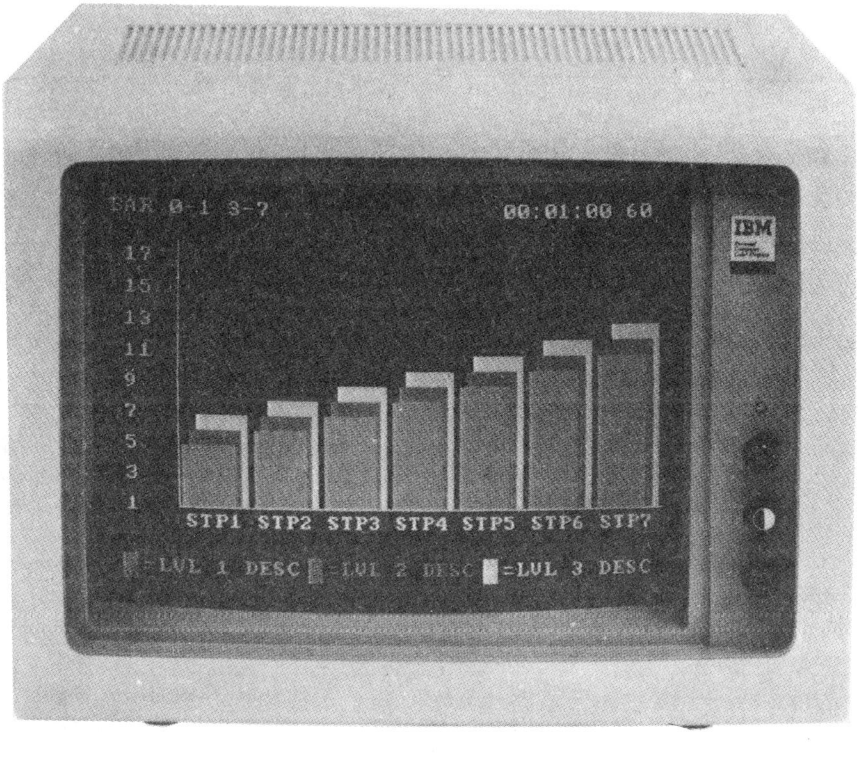

ics. While most general purpose computers have graphics software packages which can be bought by the user, the quality of microcomputer graphics is generally superior. Moreover, due to the increased use of personal computers in business, there is much more graphics software available for micros than for other types of computers. Finally, it is possible to create computer "pictures" with some microcomputers without special software and without a great deal of special training. In fact, the graphics feature is one of the microcomputer's most popular features, and has greatly contributed to its growing popularity.

MINICOMPUTERS

The minicomputer is a mid-sized computer which is much more similar 13
to the mainframe than to the micro. Like a personal computer, a minicomputer can perform many different functions. Unlike the average micro, many different users can use the minicomputer concurrently; that is, the minicomputer can serve a number of users at the same time. In addition, minicomputers can generally offer users a number of different languages to work with. Furthermore, the input, output, and the auxiliary storage

9-4 The mainframe is the largest general purpose computer and may take up as much space as an entire room.

devices for minicomputers reflect the machine's size and capability. These devices, described earlier, are larger than those used with the micro, and are the same or very similar to those used with mainframes.

MAINFRAME COMPUTERS

Finally, the mainframe is the largest general purpose computer and may 14
take up as much space as an entire room. It is likewise the most powerful general purpose computer. The mainframe is capable both of processing a great deal of data and of retrieving large amounts of data from auxiliary storage. This is because the memory of the mainframe is far larger than that of either the minicomputer or the microcomputer. Moreover, like the minicomputer, the mainframe can perform many different types of operations at the same time. The mainframe and the mini are also similar in that they both allow many different users to work at the same time. There are also a large number of different software packages available for use on mainframes. Like the minicomputer, many different computer languages are routinely used with these large machines (see below).

EXERCISES

Vocabulary from Context

A. Match the word to the correct definition. Place the number of the word in column 1 that corresponds to the correct definition in column 2. The number in parentheses indicates the paragraph in which the word can be found. Refer to the reading as necessary.

1. touch screen (8)	____ means of inputting information to the computer by speaking
2. voice input device (8)	____ a screen of a video monitor or terminal which allows information to be input simply by touching the screen with a finger
3. light pen (8)	____ input device often used to play games
4. computer keyboard (8)	____ means of input used with a light-sensitive screen
5. joystick (8)	____ input device which looks like a typewriter keyboard, but sends special signals to the computer

B. Fill in the blanks with one of the following words or terms from the reading. Refer to the indicated paragraph as necessary. Be sure to use the correct grammatical form.

versatile (3)	unique (4)	portable (6)
self-contained (6)	sensitive (8)	to configure (11)
concurrently (13)	to retrieve (14)	

1. Many users can work on a minicomputer or a mainframe ____.
2. The microcomputer is small and ____; it is easy to take it from place to place.
3. One thing a computer can do is ____ information that has been previously stored in auxiliary storage.
4. The digital computer, which is very ____, has a large number of different applications.
5. Computer systems can be set up in many different ways. They can be ____ differently.
6. A special purpose computer has a ____ application, and is therefore used for one purpose only.

7. The touch screen, which is very ____ to touch, responds immediately even to the lightest touch.
8. The personal computer is a ____ unit. It has its own CPU, input and output devices, and auxiliary storage.

C. Find each of the following words or terms in the indicated paragraph in the reading. Write a synonym, definition, or description of the word or term.

1. analog (2)
2. digital (2)
3. graphics (12)

Comprehension Exercises

A. True-False. Write a "T" if the statement is true. Write "F" if it is false.

1. The term computer refers only to the large computer which fills an entire room.
2. Both the digital and the analog computer have a large number of different applications.
3. The analog computer measures and the digital computer counts.
4. There are two types of general purpose computers—mini-computers and micros.
5. Examples of special purpose computers are air traffic systems or airline reservation systems.
6. The same basic components make up the systems of all types of general purpose computers.
7. The microcomputer is designed to be used by the average person.
8. The components of microcomputer systems can be set up in a number of different ways.
9. The only auxiliary storage available with microcomputers is a diskette.
10. Several users can work on a minicomputer at the same time.
11. A mainframe is more powerful than a minicomputer.
12. Several languages are commonly available on mainframes.

B. Choose the letter of the *best* answer for each of the following.

1. Which is *not* a characteristic of the digital computer?
   a. accuracy
   b. measurement
   c. counting by utilizing digits
   d. different applications

2. The general purpose computer ____.
   a. has a unique purpose
   b. is used only in business and education
   c. uses different software for different applications
   d. can support only one user at a time

3. The microcomputer ____.
   a. is more powerful than the minicomputer
   b. is used by computer specialists in large corporations only
   c. is used by the average person for many purposes
   d. is only good for playing games

4. Which of the following represents the most typical microcomputer system?
   a. CPU, video monitor, disk drives, keyboard
   b. CPU, joysticks, disk drives, touch screen monitor
   c. cassettes, disk drives, light pen, CPU
   d. CPU, cassettes, video monitor, disk drives

5. What is *not* a characteristic of the microcomputer?
   a. data handling
   b. one CPU for each system
   c. graphics
   d. supporting concurrent users

6. Which of the following is *not* a characteristic of the mainframe?
   a. It can perform many operations at the same time.
   b. It can support many simultaneous users.
   c. It can process large amounts of data.
   d. It can be easily transported from place to place.

Skill Enhancement

Comparison and Contrast

One of the common organizational techniques used in writing is the use of comparison and contrast. This involves determining the similarities and/or differences between two or more objects, people, ideas, situations, etc. While comparison emphasizes the similarities or common elements between things, contrast emphasizes the differences or dissimilar elements. Comparing two things really means to compare and contrast them. There must be some connection between things or they could not be compared.

There are different methods of comparing and contrasting. Two things can be compared and contrasted within the same paragraph. This can be done in two different sentences or within the same sentence.

Example (different sentences): The minicomputer is a mid-sized computer which is quite similar to the mainframe. Like the mainframe, the minicomputer can perform many different jobs at the same time.

Example (one sentence): While the mainframe and the minicomputer are very expensive, the microcomputer is generally much less expensive.

Comparisons can also be made by alternating paragraphs; one paragraph describes one thing, the next the second thing, the next paragraph returns to treat the first thing, the next paragraph deals with the second thing, etc. It is also possible to write a series of paragraphs describing one element of the comparison, followed by a second series treating the second element of the comparison, etc. This chapter combines these techniques by first comparing analog and digital computers, then dividing digital computers into special purpose and general purpose computers and comparing the two. Next general purpose computers are divided into several paragraphs dealing with microcomputers, minicomputers, and mainframes. Within each section, the computers are also compared for specific features such as size, power, types of devices used with the system, etc.

Many expressions are useful for comparing and contrasting. These special words are signals to the reader that a comparison is being made. Using such words helps the author and the reader connect clauses, sentences and paragraphs. In the following example the word "whereas" makes it clear that a contrast is being made.

Example: Whereas the microcomputer is portable, the mainframe and the minicomputer are not.

The following words and expressions are used to show similarity (comparison).

in the same way	then	accordingly	compared to
correspondingly	too	also	in comparison
equally	like	as	
as compared to	just as	similarly	

The following words and expressions are used to show differences (contrast).

whereas	unlike	on the one hand	on the other hand
yet	instead	on the contrary	in contrast (to)
despite	in spite of	conversely	although
while	however	nevertheless	different from
but	then again		

A. **Fill in the blanks with the appropriate expression of comparison or contrast based on the information in the chapter.**

The microcomputer system, ____ (like/unlike) the mainframe and minicomputer systems, consists of a CPU, input/output devices and auxiliary storage. ____, (In the same way/In contrast) because of the physical size of the microcomputer, the devices may be ____ (similar to/different from) those used with the larger computer systems. ____ (Like/Unlike) other computers, the most common input device for the personal computer is a keyboard. Many other input devices are also used with micros. ____ (Although/Just as) some of these same devices including light pens and touch screens are available for mainframes, they are not commonly used with these large computers. Finally, ____ (just as/although) different types of printers are used with micros, they are also commonly used with mainframes and minicomputers.

B. Study the following sentences of comparison and contrast. First decide whether the sentence focuses upon the similarity between things (comparison) or upon their differences (contrast). Then rewrite the sentence using another expression of comparison or contrast. You may have to add or delete words. An example has been done for you.

Example: Today, while many people still think of the large mainframe when they hear the word computer, other people immediately think of the micro.

This sentence is contrasting the old association of the term computer (mainframe) to the new association (the microcomputer).

New version of the sentence: Today, although many people still think of the large mainframe when they hear the word computer, other people immediately think of the micro.

1. Some personal computers can be quite expensive, while others may be very inexpensive.
2. Just as the mainframe is the largest and most powerful general purpose computer, it is also the most expensive.
3. Voice input devices are available today; however, they are not very common.
4. Unlike the mainframe, the microcomputer is portable.
5. In spite of its small size, the personal computer is very powerful.
6. Like the mainframe and the minicomputer, the microcomputer has a processor unit, input and output devices, and auxiliary storage units.
7. Similarly, the mainframe can support many different users concurrently.

Enrichment Activities

1. Write a composition using comparison and contrast on one of the following:
   a. Types and uses of computers in your country or school or profession
   b. The past, present, and future of computers

2. Find all the expressions of comparison and contrast in the reading passage in this chapter. Rewrite some of the sentences in the paragraph using a different expression of comparison or contrast.

3. Visit a computer store and get information about several different computers. Give an oral or written report using expressions of comparison and contrast.

CHAPTER 10

COMPUTER CODES

THE HOLLERITH CODE

As we learned in Chapter 5, the punched card (see illustration 10.1) was 1
developed in the late nineteenth century by Herman Hollerith. It is called a punched card because data is shown on the card by "punching" or making holes in certain places on the card. Machines for using the punched card were also developed at that time by Hollerith and James Powers, who also worked for the U.S. Census Bureau. Although great technological advances have been made since that time, the punched card is still important in data processing because its code—the Hollerith Code—is the basis of all modern computer codes. For this reason, the Hollerith Code will be studied in depth in this chapter.

A punched card is also called a *unit record* because each card repre- 2
sents one complete unit of information. Data are shown on a punched card according to a system developed by Herman Hollerith. This system is called the Hollerith Code. The punched card is divided into 80 vertical columns, columns that go from top to bottom. For this reason, it is also referred to as an 80-column card. The numbers 1 to 80 are written at the bottom of the card (see illustration 10.1) to show this division. Each card can hold 80 characters (numbers, letters, or symbols) of data. There are twelve horizontal rows on the punched card which go from side to side. Rows 0 to 9 are written directly on the card. Punched card users understand that rows 11 and 12 are above row 0 (see illustration 10.1). Although no numbers are written there, punched holes can be made in each of the 80 columns of rows 11 and 12. The top of the card is called the 12-edge and the bottom of the card is called the 9-edge. This fact should be remembered because in some card readers the 12-edge is put in first and in others the 9-edge is inserted first.

Rows 0 to 9 on the punched card are called *digit rows*, and rows 0, 11, 3
and 12 are called *zone rows*. Row 0, therefore, can be either a zone row or a digit row, but not both at the same time. If a digit (a single character

Computer technology affects every aspect of modern life. New applications allow business professionals to use their time more creatively in the office and at home.

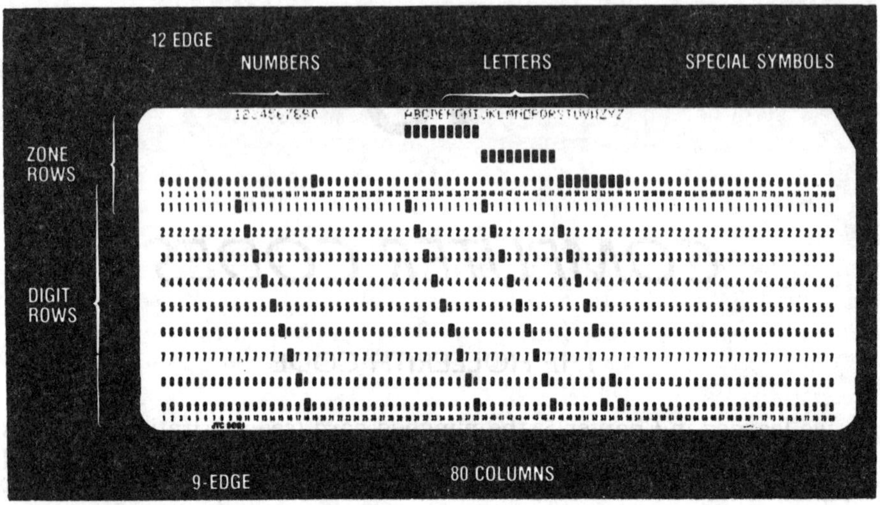

10-1 The punched card is also called a unit record.

number from 0 to 9) is needed, one rectangular punch, or hole, is made in a column. If a column has only one punch in a digit row and none in a zone row, we know that the data in that column is a number. Column 5 on the punched card in illustration 10.1 represents the number 5.

It is useful to become familiar with the Hollerith Code not only in 4
order to be able to "read" a punched card if necessary, but also because it provides a basis for the coding system used in digital computers. According to the Hollerith Code, an alphabetic character (a letter) is represented by two punches in one column; one punch is in a digit row (1 to 9), and one punch is in a zone row. The letter "A," for example (see illustration 10.1), is represented by a punch in zone row 12 and digit row 1. The code for alphabetic characters is as follows:

Letter	Zone-digit	to	Zone-digit
A to I	12–1	to	12–9
J to R	11–1	to	11–9
S to Z	0–2	to	0–9

The punches for each letter are shown in illustration 10.1. Special symbols ($, #, %, etc.) are shown by three punches, one in a zone row and two in digit rows.

A 96-column card has also been developed and is used with certain 5
IBM systems. This card is smaller than the 80-column card and can hold more data. The code used with the 96-column card is based on the Hollerith Code and is called BCD (*B*inary *C*oded *D*ecimal). We will learn more about BCD in the discussion of the binary number system.

THE BINARY SYSTEM

In an electronic digital computer the circuits can only be in one of two 6
positions: either on or off. In the same way, the magnetic cores in some main storage units can be magnetized in one of two ways: either in a clockwise or counterclockwise direction. For this reason, machine language (the most basic language of the computer) is composed of a code with only two digits (a digit is a single character number): 1 and 0. The digit 1 represents the "on" position of a circuit, and the digit 0 represents the "off" position. The number system that uses only two digits (1 and 0) is called the *binary* (the prefix bi- means "two") number system. An understanding of the binary code used for computers is essential for the computer science student.

Reviewing the way in which our own number system, the decimal 7
system (the prefix "dec" means "ten"), works will help us understand the binary system. The decimal system uses 10 digits. These ten digits are 0, 1, 2, 3, 4, 5, 6, 7, 8, and 9. Each digit in a decimal number represents that number multiplied by the number 10 raised to a certain power. That power is called an *exponent* and causes the number to be multiplied by itself as many times as the exponent indicates. Remember that any number raised to the 0 power is equal to 1. Study the following example:

$$
\begin{array}{rrrr}
354 = & 4 \times 10^0 = 4 \times 1 & = & 4 \\
 & 5 \times 10^1 = 5 \times 10 & = & 50 \\
 & 3 \times 10^2 = 3 \times 100 & = & \underline{300} \\
 & & & 354
\end{array}
$$

Another way of thinking of the value of each digit place would be the following:

10^4	10^3	10^2	10^1	10^0		
10,000	1,000	100	10	1		
5	3	7	8	2	=	50,000
						3,000
						700
						80
					+	2
						53,782

CONVERTING BINARY NUMBERS TO DECIMAL NUMBERS

In the binary number system, each digit represents that number multi- 8
plied by the number 2 raised to a certain power. Remember, however, that

in the binary system there are only 2 digits: 0 and 1. Study the following example:

$$
\begin{aligned}
101 = 1 \times 2^0 &= 1 \times 1 = 1 \\
0 \times 2^1 &= 0 \times 2 = 0 \\
1 \times 2^2 &= 1 \times 4 = \underline{4} \\
& \qquad\qquad\;\; 5
\end{aligned}
$$

Thus, the decimal equivalent of the binary number 101 is 5. Following is another way of thinking of the value of each digit place and of determining the decimal equivalent of a binary number.

2^4	2^3	2^2	2^1	2^0
16	8	4	2	1
1	1	0	1	0

$$
= \begin{array}{r} 0 \\ 2 \\ 0 \\ 8 \\ +\,16 \\ \hline 26 \end{array}
$$

Thus, the binary number 11010 (which is read one-one-zero-one-zero) is equal to the decimal number 26.

CONVERTING DECIMAL NUMBERS TO BINARY NUMBERS

Using the same system, but in reverse, we can determine the binary equiv- 9
alent of a decimal number. For example, suppose we want to find the binary equivalent of the number 873. First, we set up the values of each digit place in the binary system.

2^{10}	2^9	2^8	2^7	2^6	2^5	2^4	2^3	2^2	2^1	2^0
1,024	512	256	128	64	32	16	8	4	2	1

Second, we decide which is the highest value place which goes into the number without exceeding it, that is, without going beyond or totalling more than the original number. We place a 1 in that value place. 512 is the highest number that goes into 873 without exceeding it, so we place a 1 in that place:

2^{10}	2^9	2^8	2^7	2^6	2^5	2^4	2^3	2^2	2^1	2^0
1,024	512	256	128	64	32	16	8	4	2	1
	1									

Third, we subtract the value from the number. In this case, we subtract 512 from 873 for a new total of 361. We then repeat the steps. If the next lowest value place does not go into the new total, we place a 0 in that value place. We continue the process until we reach zero.

2^{10}	2^9	2^8	2^7	2^6	2^5	2^4	2^3	2^2	2^1	2^0
1,024	512	256	128	64	32	16	8	4	2	1
	1	1	0	1	1	0	1	0	0	1

$$\begin{array}{r} 873 \\ \underline{512} \\ 361 \\ \underline{-\ 256} \\ 105 \\ \underline{-\ \ 64} \\ 41 \\ \underline{-\ \ 32} \\ 9 \\ \underline{-\ \ \ 8} \\ 1 \\ \underline{-\ \ \ 1} \\ 0 \end{array}$$

Thus, the binary equivalent for the decimal number 873 is 1101101001.

BINARY CODES

Any decimal number can be represented in the binary number system. 10
Different codes based on the binary number system have been developed to represent not only numbers, but letters and special symbols as well. These codes are based on the binary number system, but use a number of *bits* (*B*inary dig*IT*s) which act together as a unit.

The binary number system is the basis of all these codes. The first is 11
called 4-bit BCD (*B*inary *C*oded *D*ecimal). Each group of 4 bits represents only one decimal digit. 4-bit BCD is used to represent numbers only. The second code is known as 6-bit BCD and uses 6 bits which act as a unit. The two bits which are farthest left are known as *zone bits* (the function of the zone bits in this code is similar to that of the zone rows on the punched card). The four bits to the right are known as *numeric bits* (see illustration 10.2). Numbers, upper-case (capital) letters, and special symbols, like

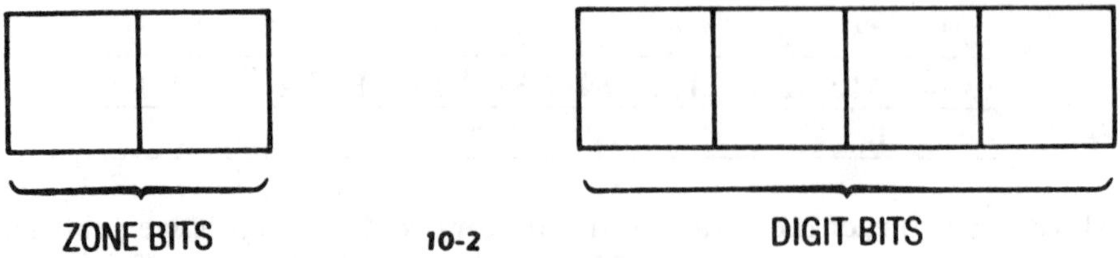

10-2

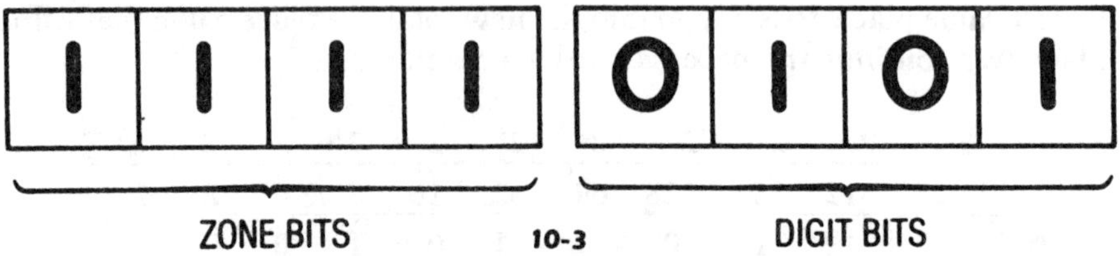

10-3

punctuation symbols, can be coded using 6-bit BCD. The third code is called EBCDIC (*E*xtended *B*inary *C*oded *D*ecimal *I*nterchange *C*ode). This is an 8-bit code that has four zone bits and four numeric bits. This code can represent numbers, upper- and lower-case letters, and special symbols, including $, &, and ". When a number is represented in EBCDIC, all the zone bits are in the "on" position, that is, they are represented by the number 1 (see illustration 10.3). If a bit is in the "off" position, it is represented by the number 0. The fourth code based on the binary number system is a 7-bit code called ASCII (*A*merican *S*tandard *C*ode for *I*nformation *I*nterchange). This is a standard code that can be used by many different computers. The fifth code is the 8-bit version of ASCII and is called ASCII-8. In addition, a 16-bit code, which is very powerful, is also used in many computers. Currently, most computers use an 8-bit or a 16-bit code.

MEMORY: BITS AND BYTES

A number of bits which work together as a unit in representing one char- 12
acter is referred to as a *byte.* (In ASCII-8 or EBCDIC one byte is equal to 8 bits.) A byte is, therefore, actually one unit of storage. The symbol K is usually used to refer to the memory capabilities of a computer. One K is actually equal to 1,024 (2 raised to the tenth power) bytes, although many people describe one K as approximately 1,000 bytes. Thus, the inexpensive microcomputer that has 4K of memory does not really have a large memory since it can only store 4,096 characters at one time. Sometimes the word *megabyte* (the prefix "mega" means very large) is used in discussing the memory size of very large computers. A megabyte is equal to 1,024,000 bytes of storage (see illustration 10.4).

Although binary code may seem difficult at first, it is really not that 13
complicated. It is helpful for computer science students to understand binary code so that they have some knowledge of machine language. In

The switches in the illustration below represent the numeral "9".

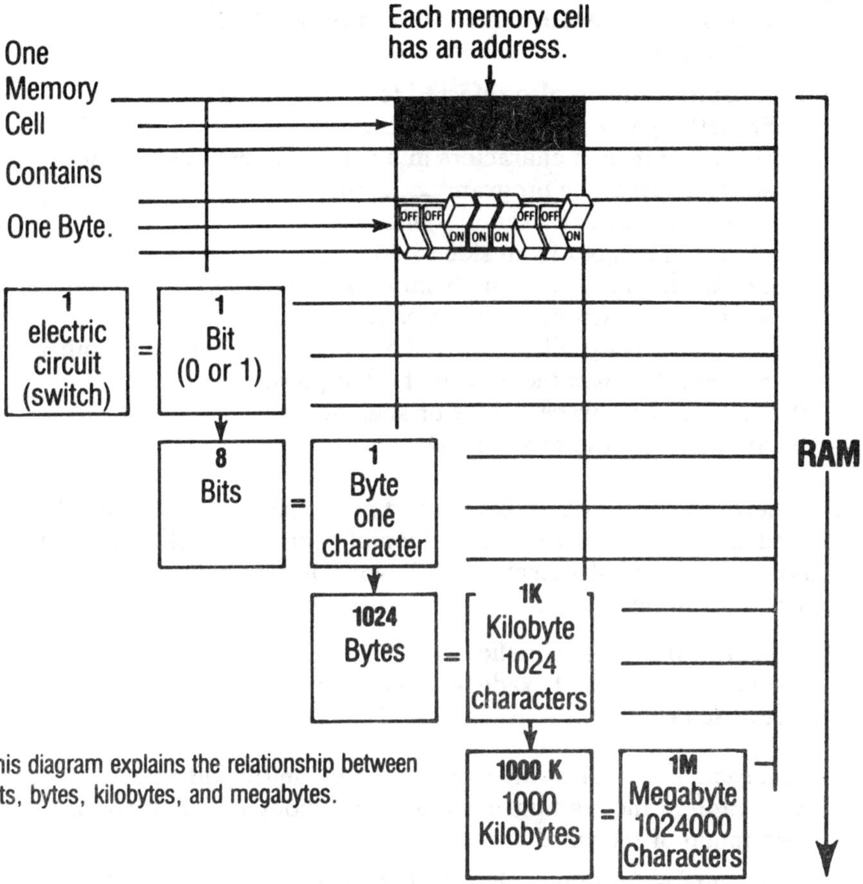

This diagram explains the relationship between bits, bytes, kilobytes, and megabytes.

addition, understanding number systems will be beneficial because some computer systems also use other number systems, like the *octal* (the prefix "oct" means eight) and the *hexadecimal* (the prefix "hex" means six) systems, in order to make program debugging easier.

EXERCISES

Vocabulary from Context

A. Fill in the blanks with one of the following words or terms from the reading. Refer to the indicated paragraph as necessary. Be sure to use the correct grammatical form.

character (2)	horizontal (2)	digit (3)
alphabetic (4)	exponent (7)	equivalent (8)
to exceed (9)	symbol (10)	upper-case (11)
complicated (13)		

1. A capital letter is also referred to as an ____ letter.
2. Something that is simple is not ____.
3. If the number of characters in a program goes beyond the storage space, the program ____ memory.
4. #, %, and * are all examples of ____.
5. A ____ line goes from side to side.
6. The decimal ____ of the binary number 10 is 2.
7. A single character number is called a ____.
8. The ____ is usually written above and to the right of another number. It raises the number to that power.
9. A ____ is a number, letter or symbol.
10. An ____ character is a letter.

B. Review the stems and affixes studied in the previous chapters. Using word analysis, try to give a definition of each of the following words. Indicate the part of speech of each word. Refer to the indicated paragraph if necessary.

1. binary (6)
2. decimal (7)
3. reverse (9)
4. beneficial (13)
5. hexadecimal (13)

C. Find each of the following words or terms in the indicated paragraph in the reading. Then write a synonym, definition, or description of the word or term.

1. 80-column card (2)
2. 9-edge (2)
3. bit (10)
4. 4-bit BCD (11)
5. EBCDIC (11)
6. ASCII (11)
7. byte (12)
8. K (12)

Comprehension Exercises

A. Choose the letter of the *best* answer for each of the following.

1. Which of the following is *not* a zone row on the punched card?
   a. 12
   b. 0
   c. 9
   d. 11

2. What is the correct punch for the letter "U"?
   a. 11–9
   b. 12–5
   c. 0–8
   d. 0–4

3. Which of the following is *not* an alphabetic character?
   a. A
   b. Z
   c. &
   d. C

4. Which number system uses only two digits?
   a. binary
   b. decimal
   c. hexadecimal
   d. none of the above

5. What number does 2^{10} represent?
   a. 64
   b. 200
   c. 1,024
   d. 20

6. EBCDIC can represent ______.
   a. only numbers
   b. numbers and symbols
   c. numbers and letters
   d. numbers, letters, and symbols

7. Which of the following codes is probably the most like EBCDIC?
   a. 4-bit BCD
   b. 6-bit BCD
   c. ASCII
   d. ASCII-8

8. Which of the following is a lower-case letter?
   a. %
   b. t
   c. 7
   d. G

9. How are numbers represented in EBCDIC?
   a. all the zone bits are "on"
   b. all the zone bits are "off"
   c. the zone bits are not used
   d. two zone bits are "on" and two are "off"

10. How many bits would be equal to 1 byte in EBCDIC?
    a. 4
    b. 6
    c. 7
    d. 8

11. How many characters can a computer with 48K of memory store?
    a. 48
    b. 384
    c. 49,152
    d. 80,000

12. How many digits does the octal number system have?
    a. 2
    b. 8
    c. 10
    d. 16

13. Why is it helpful to know binary code?
    a. because it can be changed to decimal
    b. because it is based on the Hollerith Code
    c. because it forms the basis for all machine language
    d. because it represents upper and lower case letters

B. Change the following binary numbers to decimal numbers. Use the value position chart to help you.

2^{10}	2^9	2^8	2^7	2^6	2^5	2^4	2^3	2^2	2^1	2^0
1,024	512	256	128	64	32	16	8	4	2	1

1. 1011
2. 11010
3. 11000
4. 1011011
5. 11001101

C. Change the following decimal numbers to binary numbers. Use the value position chart to help you.

2^{10}	2^9	2^8	2^7	2^6	2^5	2^4	2^3	2^2	2^1	2^0
1,024	512	256	128	64	32	16	8	4	2	1

1. 15
2. 84
3. 173
4. 410
5. 689

Skill Enhancement

Cardinal and Ordinal Numbers

In English there are two types of numbers: cardinal numbers and ordinal numbers. (Both of these are based on the decimal number system.) Both cardinal and ordinal numbers can only be used with count nouns. Ordinal numbers are formed from cardinal numbers as follows (remember that the cardinal number zero (0) has no ordinal form):

one (1)	first (1st)
two	second (2nd)
three	third (3rd)
four	fourth (4th)
five	fifth
six	sixth
seven	seventh
eight	eighth
nine	ninth
ten	tenth
eleven	eleventh
twelve	twelfth
thirteen	thirteenth
fourteen	fourteenth
fifteen	fifteenth
sixteen	sixteenth
seventeen	seventeenth
eighteen	eighteenth
nineteen	nineteenth
twenty	twentieth (20th)
twenty-one	twenty-first (21st)
thirty	thirtieth
forty	fortieth
fifty	fiftieth
sixty	sixtieth
seventy	seventieth
eighty	eightieth
ninety	ninetieth
one (a) hundred	(one, a) hundredth
two hundred	two hundredth
one (a) thousand	(one, a) thousandth
one (a) million	(one, a) millionth
one (a) billion	(one, a) billionth
one (a) trillion	(one, a) trillionth

Cardinal numbers are the numbers we commonly use for counting. Both cardinal and ordinal numbers can be used as pronouns or as adjectives, and both can be used as sequence or listing indicators (refer to Chapter 2). An ordinal number which functions as an adverb or pronoun is usually preceded by an article—in most cases, the definite article (*the* first code, etc.). Ordinal numbers are often used as temporal adjectives or adverbs. Ordinal numbers are abbreviated by writing the numeral followed by the last two letters of the number (1st, 2nd, 3rd, 4th, etc.).

The numerator (the number on top) of a fraction is always a cardinal number. The denominator (the number below the line) is an ordinal number. The only exception to this is the fraction ½, which is written one half, a half, or half. The fraction ¼ can be written as one (a) quarter or one (a) fourth.

All other denominators are written (and pronounced) as ordinal numbers. Remember that if the numerator is more than one, the ordinal number that represents the denominator must be written as a plural ($\frac{2}{6}$ = two sixths). An exponent is also expressed as an ordinal number (two to the tenth power equals 1,024). However, the term "squared" is usually used when a number is raised to the second power; the term "cubed" is often used when a number is raised to the third power.

A. Write the ordinal number and the abbreviation of the ordinal number that correspond to the following cardinal numbers.

1. 21
2. 12
3. 32
4. 100
5. 203

B. Rewrite the following sentences by writing out the numbers.

1. Magnetic tape is often ½ inch wide.
2. It can also come in a width of ¾ of an inch.
3. Sometimes magnetic tape is ⅜ of an inch wide.
4. 2^5 is equal to 32.
5. A nanosecond is 1/1,000,000,000 of second.
6. A megabyte is equal to 1,024,000 bytes of storage.

Enrichment Activities

1. On the blank punched card shown below write your name (last name first), the name of your class and today's date using the Hollerith Code. Be sure to put the printed information at the top so that people who do not know the Hollerith Code can read it.

2. Scan the reading in order to find the ordinal numbers. When a series of ordinals is used, rewrite the series using cardinal numbers.

3. The octal numbering system is based on the digits 0, 1, 2, 3, 4, 5, 6, and 7. First, complete the value position chart below for the octal numbering system. Then, using your knowledge of how number systems operate, rewrite the following decimal numbers a) in the binary numbering system and b) in the octal numbering system.

8^5	8^4	8^3	8^2	8^1	8^0
32,768		512		8	1

1. 1,087
2. 973
3. 72
4. 57
5. 16

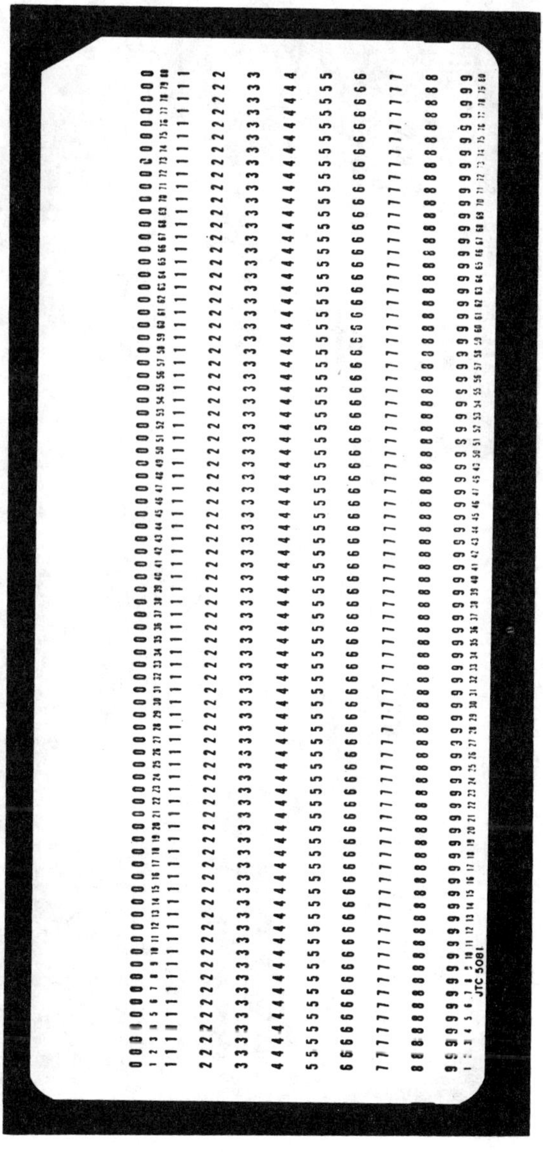

CHAPTER 11

COMPUTER LANGUAGES

Just as people use languages to communicate with each other, computer 1
languages are used to give instructions to computers. Computers don't communicate the way human beings do, however. A computer, by itself, has no creativity and cannot express ideas, emotions or desires. In fact, computers must be told exactly what to do, or they can't do anything at all. While human ideas are expressed through words and sentences, computer instructions are given to the computer with a *program,* a set of instructions arranged in a particular sequence in order to obtain a specific result. If a computer is programmed correctly, it can carry out the most complex task as easily as the simplest. In contrast, if it is programmed incorrectly, the simplest task can become a terrible problem.

TYPES OF COMPUTER LANGUAGES

Just as human beings speak different languages, computers "speak" dif- 2
ferent languages too. Computer languages are less numerous than human languages, although more than 200 languages have been developed for computers over the last 25 years. There are three levels of computer languages: 1) machine languages, which are very, very difficult; 2) low-level assembly languages, which are easier than machine languages, and 3) high-level programming languages, which are the easiest of all three types.

11-1 Computer languages are used to give instructions to computers.

MACHINE LANGUAGE

A *machine language* is the particular language of a specific computer. 3
Machine languages are written in binary code (see illustration 11.1), and are therefore really a series of binary numbers. Machine language programs work very quickly; in fact, such programs work much more rapidly than programs written in any other language. Machine language programs are also more economical than other programs in terms of storage space. However, the same qualities which make machine languages fast and economical also make them difficult to master. For example, we have already stated that writing programs in machine language consists of writing binary code; binary code is very hard to use. In addition, machine language is machine-dependent, that is, able to be used only on one specific computer. This means that programs written in machine language must be modified for every computer.

SYMBOLIC COMPUTER LANGUAGES

In contrast to machine language, there is another level of computer lan- 4
guage—*symbolic language.* Symbolic languages do not use numbers (binary code) as machine languages do. Instead they use a type of code—*special symbols*—to represent numbers and give instructions to the computer. Programs written in symbolic languages are much easier to read and write than those written in machine language.

ASSEMBLY LANGUAGES

There are two types of symbolic languages: low-level assembly languages, 5
and high-level programming languages. *Assembly languages* are called low-level languages because they are closer to machine language than programming languages are. Assembly languages are machine-dependent and are, therefore, almost as closely related to the computer as machine language. Like programs written in machine language, assembly language programs are efficient for the programmer to write. They are easier to write than machine language programs, but are still more difficult than programs written in high-level programming languages. They are also economical in terms of storage space and are executed quickly.

PROGRAMMING LANGUAGES

Although assembly languages are widely used, high-level *programming* 6
languages are more popular than any other type of computer language. Programming languages are called high-level languages because they are

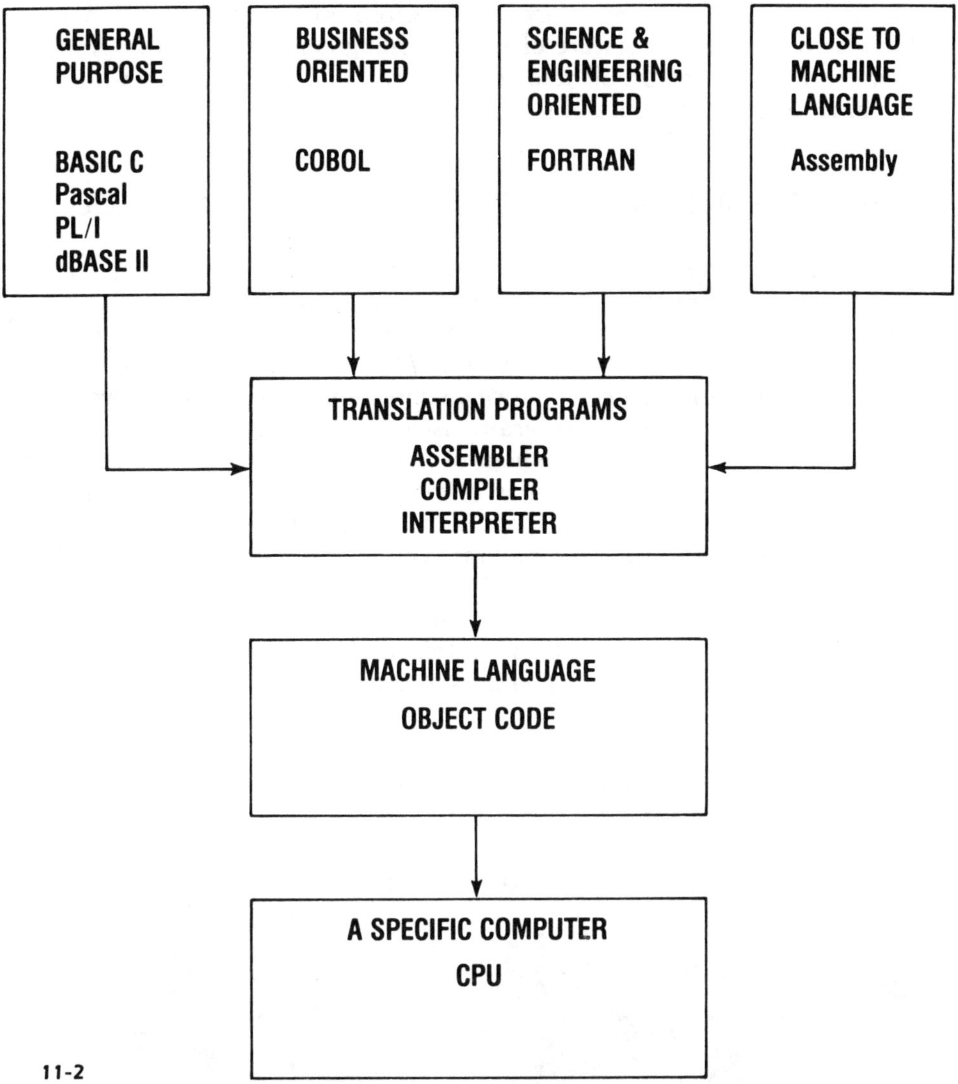

11-2

Reprinted from *Through the Micromaze; A Visual Guide from Ashton-Tate,* by W. Creekmore. © 1983 Ashton-Tate. All Rights Reserved.

close to human language. They were invented to make programming as easy as possible. The *statements,* the actual written lines, in programs written in programming languages are not as related to the characteristics of a particular computer as are those of assembly or machine languages. In fact, programming languages are much more universal than either assembly or machine languages. They are therefore much easier to use. Also, because of the general nature of programming languages, the programmer can focus on the problem to be solved without having to worry about the internal characteristics of the computer.

TRANSLATING PROGRAMS INTO MACHINE LANGUAGE

Program instructions written in machine language are immediately car- 7
ried out by the computer. Programs written in assembly or programming languages are not. Programs written in either assembly or programming languages are called *source programs.* All source programs must go through a translation process and be changed into binary code before the computer can carry out the program instructions (see illustration 11.2).

There are two common methods of translating source programs into 8
binary code. One method, popular in microcomputers, is the use of an *interpreter,* a special program stored in the computer's memory. An interpreter reads one statement of a program and then executes that particular statement.

The other common method of translating source programs is used by 9
mainframe and minicomputers. With this method, each statement is not executed one after the other as with an interpreter. Instead a special pro-

11-3 An interactive language is one which is more communicative than other programming languages.

gram translates the entire source program at once. The translator for assembly languages is called an *assembler;* the translator for programming languages is called a *compiler.* Assemblers and compilers do exactly the same thing—they translate the entire source program into binary code. Once the source program has been translated it is called by a new name; it is called an *object program.* With this method, an object program must be created before the computer can carry out the program instructions.

PROGRAMMING LANGUAGES

There are many different programming languages. Most programming 10
languages can be used for different applications, although some are better designed for specific uses than are others. Many programming languages have long and complicated names which are usually reduced to acronyms. These include ALGOL (*ALGO*rithmic *L*anguage), a language generally used for scientific programming, and APL (*A P*rogramming *L*anguage), used mainly for mathematical applications. Another widely used language is PL/I (*P*rogramming *L*anguage/*I*), a powerful language used in both business and scientific fields. Other programming languages have been named for famous people such as Pascal, a general purpose language named for Blaise Pascal, or Ada, the U.S. Defense Department's language, named for Ada Lovelace. There are literally hundreds more programming languages, including BASIC, COBOL, and FORTRAN, which are currently among the most popular and frequently used languages. We will now examine several of these languages.

BASIC

BASIC stands for *B*eginner's *A*ll-purpose *S*ymbolic *I*nstruction *C*ode. It 11
was developed in 1965 at Dartmouth College by Dr. John Kemeny and Dr. Thomas Kurtz. BASIC was originally designed to be used by college students in many fields. It was also designed to be easier and more versatile than other, more scientific languages. In addition, BASIC was designed as an interactive language. An *interactive language* is one which is much more communicative than other types of programming languages. That is, an interactive language allows interaction—a type of conversation—between the computer and the user both during the preparation of programs and their execution. In fact, with BASIC the user and the computer alternate "talking" to each other as the program progresses (see illustration 11-3).

BASIC is much less complicated than other programming languages. 12
As it is easier and friendlier than many other languages, BASIC is the most frequently used programming language among the general population. BASIC is also very popular today because microcomputers use it as their

main language. In additon, BASIC is almost always available on mainframe and minicomputer systems, although it may be used less often than the other languages available. In fact, BASIC continues to become more and more popular every day especially for personal and educational uses.

FORTRAN

Another language that is very widely used is FORTRAN. FORTRAN stands 13
for *FOR*mula *TRAN*slation and was first developed by IBM from 1954–1957. It has since gone through several revisions, and was put into a final and standard form in 1977. FORTRAN is more complicated and structured than BASIC and is generally harder to master. It is not designed for interactive purposes, but to express mathematical calculations and scientific formulas as easily and as accurately as possible. FORTRAN instructions are stated in a combination of English and algebraic formulas. FORTRAN is better suited for work with numbers than any other programming language, and is therefore the most commonly employed language in the scientific and mathematical fields.

COBOL

COBOL, the acronym for *CO*mmon *B*usiness *O*riented *L*anguage, is the 14
best and most popular of all programming languages which have business applications. COBOL was first released in 1960 and was developed to fulfill the needs of both businesses and government. It has been revised and improved several times, and its present form was approved in 1974. A new version is scheduled to be released in the 1980s. COBOL is more similar to English than either FORTRAN or BASIC. In fact, statements in COBOL are so English-like that they are quite easy to read because they use English verbs such as read, write, add, or subtract to express computer functions.

PASCAL

Finally, a more recently developed programming language is Pascal. Pas- 15
cal, which was first used in the early 1970s, is not an acronym like BASIC or FORTRAN. Rather, Pascal was named for Blaise Pascal, the developer of one of the earliest calculating machines. Pascal, a multipurpose language, can be used for many different applications. Pascal is becoming very popular today. In fact, many people feel it will one day be more commonly used for programming microcomputers than BASIC.

EXERCISES

Vocabulary from Context

A. Match the word to the correct definition. Place the number of the word in column 1 that corresponds to the correct definition in column 2. The number in parentheses indicates the paragraph in which the word can be found. Refer to the reading as necessary.

1. program (1)	____	language of a particular computer which can be executed without being translated
2. machine language (3)	____	translator for assembly language
3. symbolic language (4)	____	source program that has been compiled or assembled
4. source program (7)	____	set of instructions in a specific sequence designed to solve a particular problem
5. assembler (9)	____	translator for high-level programming languages
6. programming language (6)	____	means of executing programs without creating object programs
7. compiler (9)	____	written line in a program
8. interpreter (8)	____	language which represents numbers with symbols
9. object program (9)	____	FORTRAN or COBOL are examples
10. statement (6)	____	program before it has been translated

B. Fill in the blanks with one of the following words or terms from the reading. Refer to the indicated paragraph as necessary. Be sure to use the correct grammatical form.

numerous (2)	to master (3)	universal (6)
interactive (11)	to alternate (11)	standard (13)
version (14)	multipurpose (15)	

1. Some programming languages can be used on any type of computer. They are not machine-dependent; they are ____.
2. Computer languages are so ____ that more than 200 have been counted.

3. There were several _____ of FORTRAN before a final form of the language was developed.
4. BASIC, an _____ language, allows the user and the computer to communicate with each other in a type of conversation.
5. PL/I, a _____ language, is used for applications in several different fields.
6. Some programming languages were changed and improved several times before a final form was decided upon and the final _____ was approved.
7. A user and the computer take turns "talking" to each other in BASIC. They have a conversation and each _____ talking to the other.
8. Machine language is difficult to learn very well. It is difficult _____.

C. Write the acronyms for the following.

1. Beginner's All-purpose Symbolic Instruction Code
2. Formula Translation
3. Common Business Oriented Language
4. Algorithmic Language

Comprehension Exercises

A. True-False. Write a "T" if the statement is true. Write "F" if it is false.

1. There are only seven computer languages used for programming.
2. A program written in machine language must be translated by an assembler.
3. Programs written in machine language have to be different for every computer.
4. Assembly languages are also called low-level languages because they are closely related to the internal characteristics of the computer.
5. Programming languages were developed to help people program computers more easily.
6. The translator for high-level languages is the assembler.
7. Interpreters are commonly used in microcomputers.
8. BASIC is the language most commonly used in the scientific field.
9. COBOL is very well suited to business applications.
10. FORTRAN has its major use in science.
11. A programming language named for a famous person is Ada.

B. Choose the letter of the *best* answer for each of the following.

1. In general, computer programs _____.
   a. are very creative instructions for the computer

b. are specific series of instructions for the computer
c. can achieve their results even if the information given to the computer is wrong
d. are written in English

2. Which is *not* a characteristic of programs written in machine language?
   a. They are machine-dependent.
   b. They are a series of numbers.
   c. They are very economical and efficient.
   d. They are very easy to read and write.

3. Programs written in symbolic languages ____.
   a. are written in binary code
   b. use symbols which are translated to numbers
   c. use symbols which are immediately understood and executed by the computer
   d. are more difficult to read than programs in machine language

4. Which is *not* true of programs written in assembly languages?
   a. They are close to machine language.
   b. They are very easy to write.
   c. They are translated by an assembler.
   d. They are not as efficient as programs written in high-level programming languages.

5. Which of the following is *not* a programming language?
   a. PL/I
   b. ALGOL
   c. PASCE
   d. FORTRAN

Skill Enhancement

Comparison of Adjectives and Adverbs

One way to describe two or more things is to compare them using adjectives and adverbs. Adjectives and adverbs have both comparative and superlative forms. The comparative form is used to compare two things; the superlative is used to compare three or more things.

Adjectives are compared in the following manner:

A. Comparative of adjectives: Formation

1. Adjectives of one syllable form the comparative by adding **-er**.
   adjective + **er**: hard → harder

   Two-syllable adjectives ending in consonant **-y** form the comparative by changing **-y** to **-i** and adding **-er**: happy → happier

Two-syllable adjectives ending in **-ow** form the comparative by adding **-er:** narrow → narrower

2. Other adjectives of two or more syllables form the comparative by placing **more** before the adjective.

   more + *adjective:* difficult → more difficult

B. Comparative of Adjectives: Structures

1. Comparisons of equality have the following structure:
   as + *adjective* + **as**
   FORTRAN is as easy as COBOL.

2. Affirmative statements of inequality for the comparative have the following structures:
   adjective + **er** + **than**
   Assembly languages are harder than programming languages.

   more + *adjective* + **than**
   Assembly languages are more difficult than programming languages.

3. Negative statements (inequality) compare with the following structures:
   not as + *adjective* + **as** *or* **not so** + *adjective* + **as**
   Programming languages are not as (so) hard as assembly languages.

4. Negative comparisons (inequality) of longer adjectives are usually made with the following structure:
   less + *adjective* + **than**
   Programming languages are less difficult than assembly languages.

5. A great difference can be indicated by adding the word much:
   much + *adjective* + **er** + **than**
   much + **more** + *adjective* + **than**
   Assembly languages are much harder (more difficult) than programming languages.

C. Superlative of Adjectives: Formation

To compare three or more things, use the superlative form of the adjective.

1. Adjectives of one syllable form the superlative by adding **-est**.
   adjective + **est**: hard → hardest

   Two syllable adjectives ending in **-y** form the superlative by changing **-y** to **-i** and adding **-est**: happy → happiest.

   Two syllable adjectives ending in **-ow** form the superlative by adding **-est**: narrow → narrowest

2. Other adjectives of two or more syllables form the superlative by adding **most** before the adjective.
   most + *adjective:* difficult → most difficult

D. Superlative of Adjectives: Structure

1. Superlative structures usually include the definite article "the" before the adjective. A complement generally follows the superlative form to further describe the class the item belongs to. The complement is usually a prepositional phrase with *of* or *in*.
   the + *adjective* + (of . . .)
   Machine languages are the hardest (of all computer languages).

   the + **most** + *adjective* + (of . . .)
   Machine languages are the most difficult (of all computer languages).

2. The initial complement after a superlative may be followed by other complements including another prepositional phrase, a participial phrase, or an adjective clause.

   Machine languages are the hardest (of all computer languages that are taught in this class).

11-4 The growing popularity of personal computers is shown by their increased use for such household tasks as projecting budgets and balancing checkbooks.

3. Negative comparisons in the superlative are usually made with this structure:
the + **least** + *adjective* + (of . . .)
Programming languages are the least difficult (of all computer languages).

E. Irregular forms of adjectives in the comparative and the superlative include:

good	→ better	→ the best
bad	→ worse	→ the worst
farther	→ farther	→ the farthest
much	→ more	→ the most
many	→ more	→ the most
little	→ less	→ the least

F. Comparison of Adverbs: Formation

1. Adverbs with the same form as adjectives are formed by adding **-er** or **-est**.

adverb + **er**: hard → harder
adverb + **est**: hard → hardest

This is also true of adverbs of time, such as late, early, and soon.
adverb + **er**: late → later
adverb + **est**: late → latest

2. Adverbs of manner ending in **-ly**.
The comparative is formed with the following structure:
more + *adverb*: efficiently → more efficiently
The superlative is formed with the following structure:
most + *adverb*: efficiently → most efficiently

G. Comparative and Superlative of Adverbs: Structure

1. Comparisons of equality are formed with the following structure:
as + *adverb* + **as**
COBOL works as efficiently as FORTRAN.

2. Affirmative statements of inequality for the comparative and superlative of adverbs have the following structures:
Comparative: **more** + *adverb* + **than**
Assembly languages work more efficiently than programming languages.

Superlative: **the** + **most** + *adverb* + (of . . .)
Machine languages work the most efficiently (of all computer languages).

Other complements may follow the initial complement of a

superlative structure, or be omitted, as with the superlative of adjectives.
Machine languages work the most efficiently (of all computer languages that are used today).

3. Negative statements of inequality for the comparative and superlative of adverbs have the following structure:

   comparative: **not** + **as** + *adverb* + **as**
   Programming languages do not work as efficiently as assembly languages.

   comparative: **less** + *adverb* + **than**
   Programming languages work less efficiently than assembly languages.

   superlative: **the least** + *adverb* + (of . . .)
   Programming languages work the least efficiently (of all computer languages).

H. Irregular forms of adverbs in the comparative and superlative include:

well →	better	→ the best
badly →	worse	→ the worst
much →	more	→ the most
———	less	→ the least
far →	farther	→ the farthest

EXERCISES

A. Fill in the blanks in the paragraph using the correct form of the word in parentheses. Use any other words you might need to make the comparison. The paragraph is similar to the reading passage. Refer to the reading only if necessary. The first example has been done for you.

BASIC was designed to be easier (easy) and ____ (versatile) than other, ____ (scientific), languages. BASIC was also designed as an interactive language, one which is much ____ (communicative) other types of programming languages. In addition, BASIC is much ____ (complicated) other programming languages. As it is ____ (easy) and ____ (friendly) other languages, BASIC is ________ (frequently used) programming language among the general population. BASIC is also ____ (popular) ever because microcomputers use it as their main language. In addition, BASIC is almost always available on mainframe systems, although it may be used ____ (frequently) the other languages available. In fact, BASIC continues to become ____ (popular) every day, especially for personal and educational uses.

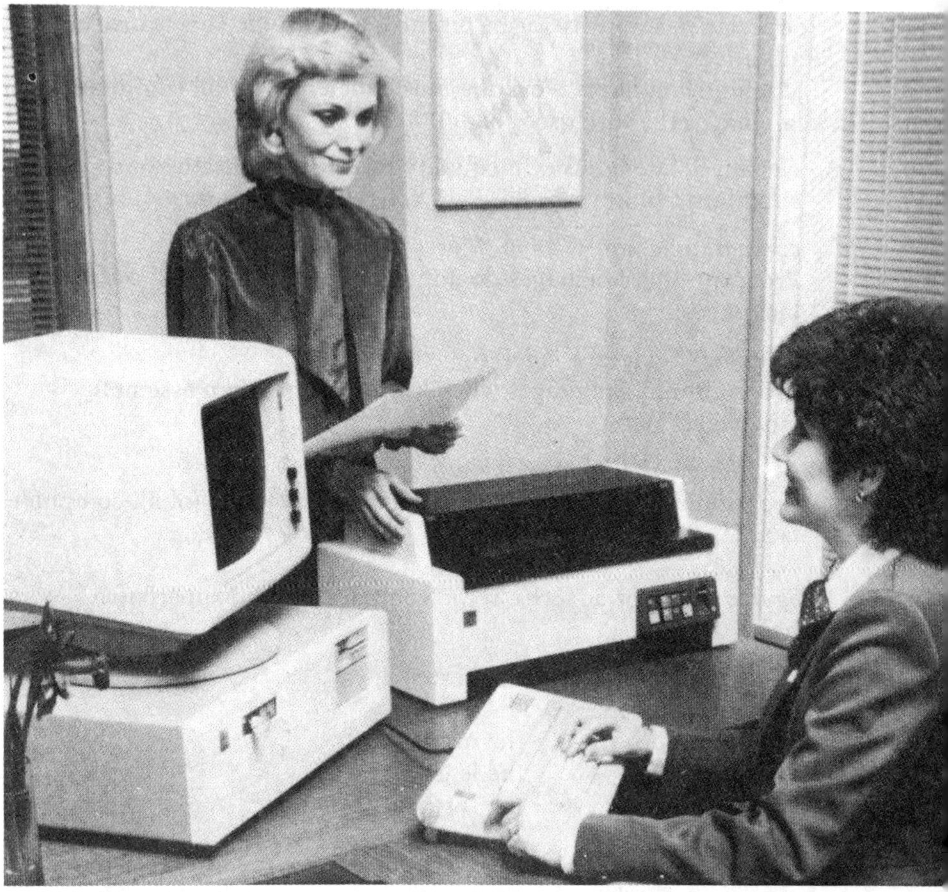

B. Write sentences using the information in this chapter and one of the structures used to compare adjectives and adverbs explained above.

Form the comparison with the first item at the beginning of the sentence.

Example: BASIC / Pascal (popular)
BASIC is more popular than Pascal.

1. Machine languages/symbolic languages (hard to learn)
2. High-level programming languages/assembly languages (easy to learn)
3. Assembly languages/high-level languages (efficient and economical)
4. BASIC/FORTRAN (popular for education)
5. FORTRAN/COBOL (express formulas accurately)
6. COBOL/FORTRAN (good for business)

C. Form the comparison with the second item at the beginning of the sentence. These are the same examples as in part B above.

Example: BASIC/Pascal (popular)
Pascal is not as popular as BASIC. *or* Pascal is less popular than BASIC.

1. Machine languages/symbolic languages (hard to learn)
2. High-level programming languages/assembly languages (easy to learn)
3. BASIC/FORTRAN (popular for education)
4. FORTRAN/COBOL (express formulas accurately)
5. COBOL/FORTRAN (good for business)

D. Form the comparison with the first item at the beginning of the sentence. Then write a sentence using the superlative.

Example: BASIC/ALGOL/Pascal (popular)
BASIC is more popular than ALGOL or Pascal. BASIC is the most popular.

1. COBOL/FORTRAN/BASIC (commonly used in business)
2. BASIC/COBOL/FORTRAN (communicative)
3. High-level programming languages/assembly languages/machine languages (difficult to master)
4. Machine languages/assembly languages/programming languages (are easily learned)

Enrichment Activities

1. Present an oral or written report comparing programming languages based on the information in the chapter. Be sure to describe the languages using comparatives and superlatives.

2. Describe how computers are used in your country as compared to the U.S. Use the comparative and superlative of adjectives and adverbs in your analysis.

USA

CHAPTER

12

PROGRAM LOGIC AND FLOWCHARTING

Computers can't do anything without being programmed correctly. Pro- 1
grams, as mentioned previously, can be written in a variety of different languages. However, it is important to remember that while computers are very powerful, they are unable to think or find solutions to problems. Instead, people think creatively, find solutions to problems, and then the computer carries them out. For these reasons, programs must be carefully planned so that the computer can accomplish the desired task. Computer programs should anticipate, that is, plan for, all the possible problems the computer might have. The program also has to be written in a very concise and exact form so that the computer can understand the instructions and implement them, that is, carry them out.

PLANNING THE PROGRAM: THE PROGRAM DEVELOPMENT CYCLE

A programmer, whether creating a very long and complex program or a 2
relatively short and simple program, should not write a program without carefully thinking about it first. In fact, before a program is written, the programmer should follow some general procedures. These steps are often called the program development cycle. Whether the particular program being written is intended for a personal computer or a mainframe, following the general procedures of the program development cycle

Space exploration would be impossible without computers which control the operation of the spacecraft as well as provide data to the astronauts.

should assist the programmer in writing a successful program. The program development cycle consists of the following stages:

1. analyzing the problem and reviewing the program requirements
2. designing the program
3. coding or writing the program
4. testing the program
5. developing documentation for the program

ANALYZING THE PROBLEM AND REVIEWING THE PROGRAM REQUIREMENTS

The first stage of the program development cycle is that of analyzing the 3
program and reviewing the program requirements. In this stage, the programmer should examine *all* aspects of the problem to be programmed. The programmer has to understand the output that is desired, the input that is needed, and the various processing procedures that must take place. For example, if a programmer is going to write a program to calculate grades or grade averages, many things, including the form of the grades (e.g., numbers or letters), whether the grades will have an equal value, or whether some assignments will be worth more than others, should be decided at this stage. During this stage of the program development cycle, the programmer should also decide which language will be used to code the program. Finally, the logic used to create the program and the structure of the program itself must be decided.

DESIGNING THE PROGRAM

The second step in the program development cycle is that of designing the 4
program. At this stage, the logic of the program should be put into a pictorial form. That is, at this point the programmer must try to picture all the small steps that are necessary to carry out the desired procedures. To do this, the programmer often creates a *flowchart,* a diagram made up of geometrical symbols that illustrates how the problem will be solved (see illustration 12.1). At this stage, then, the programmer would write a flowchart for the grade-calculating program mentioned above. Although a flowchart is not the only method of designing a program, it is still the most common. Flowcharting will be discussed later in this chapter.

CODING THE PROGRAM

The next step in the program development cycle is that of *coding* the pro- 5
gram. This is the actual writing of the program in a form the computer can understand. Proper and accurate coding is very important and must be done so that a program can be easily understood or modified. Any

appropriate computer language, like the ones discussed previously in this book, can be used for coding the program. However, it is important to remember that some languages are better and more efficient for writing programs in particular fields, as is FORTRAN for math and science. Because the problem described above is fairly simple, the programmer might choose to write the program in a general purpose language such as BASIC.

After the program is written, it should be input into the computer. 6
Once it is in the computer, a printed copy called a *listing* can then be obtained. The listing can help the programmer review the program for errors in input, typing, logic, etc. Whether or not a listing is used, reviewing small parts of a program at this point—before testing the entire program—may prove to be very helpful in creating a successful program.

TESTING THE PROGRAM

The next step in the program development cycle is that of *testing* and 7
debugging—correcting or revising—the entire program. During this stage of development, the programmer looks for and corrects additional errors in the program not found during the inputting stage. The errors are usually of two main types: problems caused by the incorrect use of a programming language; or problems caused by faulty, or incorrect, logic and program design. The testing of a program does not have to involve the use of all the data. Instead, testing can be carried out with samples of data. For example, referring to the grade program mentioned above, the testing of the program can be done with only three or four instead of fifteen or twenty actual grades. If the program works well with a small number of items, it usually works as successfully for a larger number of data items. Furthermore, although only a small number of data are used, the testing procedure must make sure that all instructions in the program are executed at least once, perhaps several times. If this is done, the programmer can be sure that all parts of the program work correctly. For the grade program this might require going through the following steps: asking for grades, inputting grades, adding the grades, dividing the total by the number of grades entered, and printing out the final grade.

DEVELOPING DOCUMENTATION FOR THE PROGRAM

After the program has been tested, the last step in the program develop- 8
ment cycle should be implemented. This is the development of documentation, detailed accounts which explain and clarify the program. Documentation should include two types of explanations: those within the program; and those written separately, often put together in book form. This type of document or book is generally called a *manual*. Creating a manual is especially important for very long and complicated programs.

FLOWCHART FOR STUDENT'S TOTAL GRADE POINTS

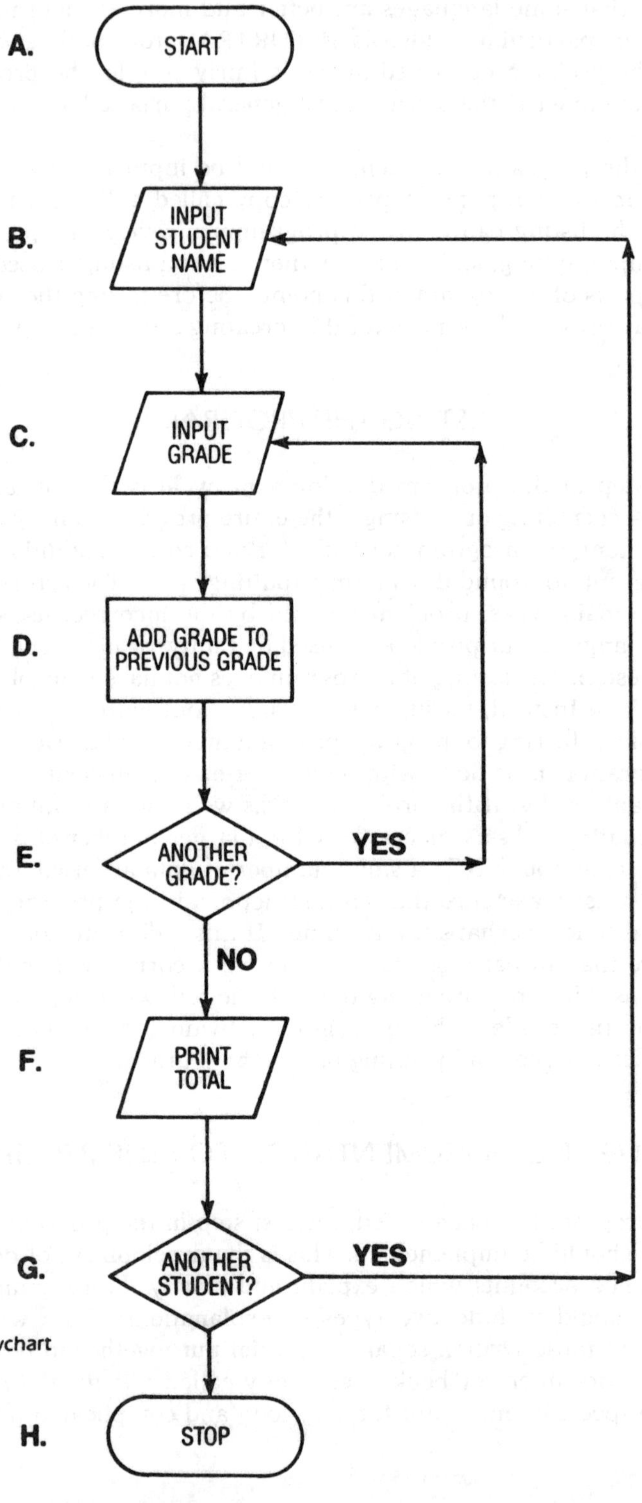

12-1 Flowchart

FLOWCHART TO FIND AVERAGE OF THREE NUMBERS

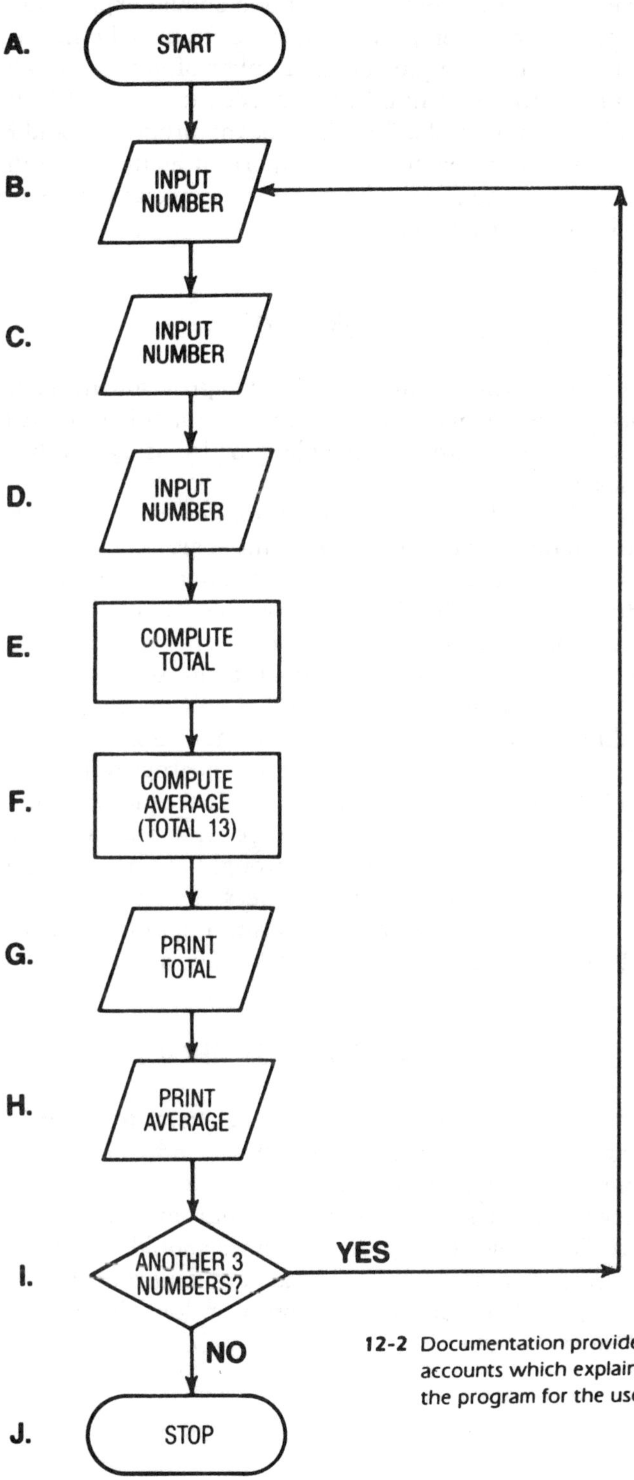

12-2 Documentation provides detailed accounts which explain and clarify the program for the user.

The documentation should explain everything possible about the program including how the program runs and what type of data is needed. For our sample grade program, the documentation should explain such things as: whether letter or number grades must be input; whether a person can calculate the average of a particular number of grades; or whether he or she may specify the total number of grades to be input in the program itself. Finally, a listing and a flowchart of the program could be included. All these materials are particularly important as they help the programmer in rewriting or modifying the program, especially if the program was developed by another person.

FLOWCHARTS

As already stated, the second step in the program development cycle 9
involves designing the logic of a program. This should be done before writing the program by creating a flowchart or by using another method of program design.

The flowchart, also called the *program flowchart* or *block diagram,* is 10
the most common method of outlining the logic of a program. The flowchart was first invented by John von Neumann at the Princeton University Institute for Advanced Studies. The flowchart is really a diagram composed of symbols, directional lines, and information about how the computer will be used to solve a particular problem (see illustration 12.2). The flowchart illustrates the steps required for solving the problem. It shows what should be done, not how it should be accomplished.

The flowchart is a very important tool for programmers and can min- 11
imize the chances of programming errors. It should not only present the logical elements of a program, but also provide a detailed plan to aid in writing the program. The flowchart also ought to serve as a means of communication between different programmers. Sometimes, if the program is very large and complex, the entire program might be divided into several small parts. In this case, each part should have a different flowchart.

FLOWCHART SYMBOLS

The flowchart is composed of symbols which refer to specific functions of 12
the computer. There should be an explanatory note in each symbol. These notes help to clarify which process should take place at each point in the entire procedure. The symbols in the flowchart are connected by *flowlines* which look like arrows (>). The flowlines should indicate the direction of the program; that is, they should indicate the order in which the steps will be executed. The normal direction of a flow should be from left to right and top to bottom.

The flowchart symbols which indicate the different computer func- 13
tions are really geometrical shapes. The most commonly used symbols are the oval, the parallelogram, the rectangle, and the diamond. A horizontal oval figure ⬭ in a flowchart is called a *terminal symbol* and must represent the starting or ending point of a program. A *parallelogram* ▱ should be used to represent either input or output. A *rectangle* ▭ is used to indicate that some kind of processing is taking place, such as adding numbers or moving data from secondary to main storage. Finally, a *diamond* ◇ is the symbol that should be used in flowcharting to indicate that a decision must be made.

Other symbols may also be used in program flowcharts. These 14
include:

=	equal to	>=	greater than or equal to
≠	not equal to	<=	less than or equal to
>	greater than	Y	Yes
<	less than	N	No

DRAWING FLOWCHARTS

A program flowchart must be simple and easy to read. Flowcharts may be 15
drawn in several ways, including by hand, or with a template. A *template* is a piece of plastic which contains the cutouts for all the flowcharting symbols (see illustration 12.3). The template can be used to trace the symbols neatly and clearly. In addition, some flowcharts can even be drawn by computers.

BREAKING DOWN THE STEPS OF A COMMON ACTION IN ORDER TO SEE HOW FLOWCHARTS ARE PLANNED

As stated, before a programmer makes a flowchart, he or she must analyze 16
a problem and break the problem down into small and logical steps. Once the problem has been broken down into its different parts, the programmer can draw a flowchart, and then use the flowchart to write a program. In order to understand how a programmer plans a program and writes a flowchart, let's break down a common action, in this case, crossing the street, into its different parts. We will not write a flowchart for "crossing the street" because this is not a process that can be carried out by the computer. However, once we see how a process can be analyzed and broken into parts, we will be able to write a flowchart for an action that can be carried out by a computer: finding and printing the average of three numbers.

STEPS IN "CROSSING THE STREET"

In order to cross the street it is necessary to do the following things:

A. Arrive at the intersection
B. Look at the traffic light
C. If the light is green, make sure the road is clear
D. If the road is clear, cross the street
E. If the light is red or yellow, wait until the light changes to green, and then repeat steps C and D.

As can be seen, what appears to be a single action is really a series of 17
separate steps. Although this activity can be broken down into small parts, it is not an activity that can be programmed for a computer. Therefore, let us now look at a flowchart for a task that can be computerized, finding the average of several numbers.

FLOWCHART FOR A COMPUTER TASK: AVERAGING NUMBERS

The preceding diagram (see illustration 12.2) illustrates a flowchart for 18
finding and printing the total and the average of three numbers. The letters on the side are not part of the flowchart, but are for explanation only. The terminal symbol in step A signals the beginning of the flowchart. The next step, step B, requests a number to be input. The request for a number to be input is repeated two more times in steps C and D so that a total of three numbers are input. Next, the total of the numbers is calculated in step E; the average is calculated in step F. The total is printed in step G and the average is printed in step H. Then a decision is required in step I; if the process is to be repeated for three more grades, the chart returns to step B and asks for more numbers to be input. If the process is not to be repeated, then step J signals the end of the program.

Writing a successful program requires the programmer to follow a 19
series of detailed steps, including analyzing the problem, designing, coding, and testing the program, and developing documentation. As we have seen, using a flowchart is a very effective and popular method of designing a program, and is an important part of developing good software.

12-3 A template is a piece of plastic which contains cutouts for all of the flowcharting symbols.

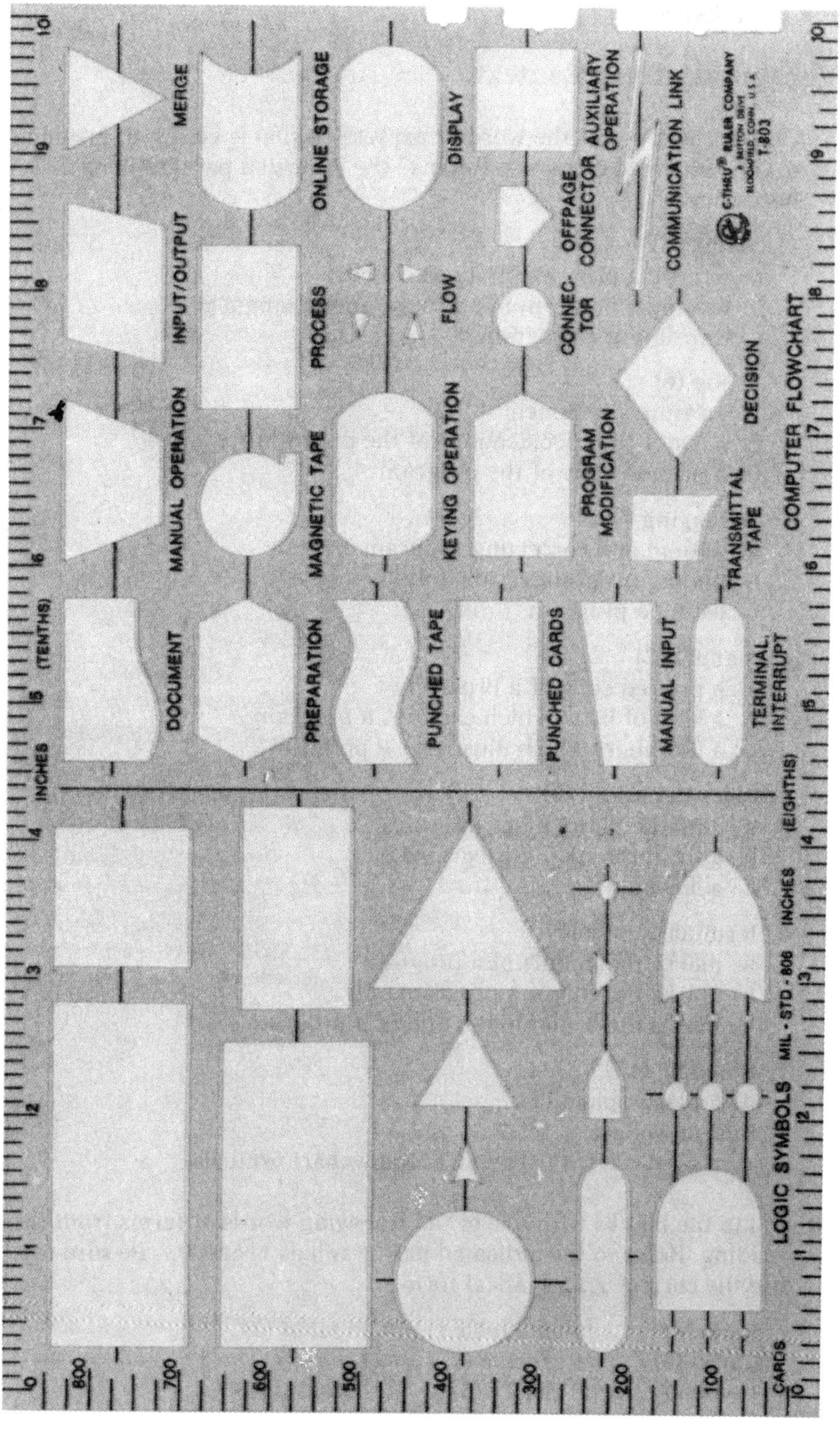
COMPUTER FLOWCHART
LOGIC SYMBOLS
MIL-STD-806
INCHES (TENTHS)
INCHES (EIGHTHS)
CARDS
MERGE
INPUT/OUTPUT
MANUAL OPERATION
DOCUMENT
ONLINE STORAGE
PROCESS
MAGNETIC TAPE
PREPARATION
DISPLAY
FLOW
KEYING OPERATION
PUNCHED TAPE
AUXILIARY OPERATION
OFFPAGE CONNECTOR
CONNEC-TOR
PROGRAM MODIFICATION
PUNCHED CARDS
COMMUNICATION LINK
DECISION
TRANSMITTAL TAPE
MANUAL INPUT
TERMINAL, INTERRUPT
C-THRU RULER COMPANY
T-803

EXERCISES

Vocabulary from Context

A. Choose the letter of the word or expression that is closest in meaning to the first word or words. Refer to the indicated paragraph as necessary.

1. coding (5)
   a. writing a program in a secret code
   b. writing a program in a programming language
   c. translating a program
2. listing (6)
   a. a printed document
   b. a list of the specifications of the program
   c. a printed copy of the program
3. debugging (7)
   a. finding and correcting program errors
   b. finding program errors only
   c. listing a program
4. manual (8)
   a. a printed copy of a program
   b. a kind of book which explains a program
   c. a flowchart which illustrates a program
5. block diagram (10)
   a. a mathematics diagram
   b. a form for coding programs
   c. a flowchart
6. terminal symbol (13)
   a. marks the middle of a program
   b. marks the end of a program only
   c. marks the beginning or end of a program
7. template (15)
   a. a plastic plate
   b. a flowchart
   c. a plastic form used to trace flowchart symbols

B. Fill in the blanks with one of the following words or terms from the reading. Refer to the indicated paragraph as necessary. Be sure to use the correct grammatical form.

creatively (1)	to anticipate (1)	to assist (2)
pictorial (4)	to execute (7)	faulty (7)
to revise (7)	to clarify (8)	cutouts (15)

1. A programmer should try _____ all the problems that he or she might encounter and plan for them in the program.
2. The program development cycle is a tool which _____ the programmer in writing successful programs.
3. Testing a program involves looking for mistakes caused by _____ logic or improper coding of the programming language.
4. After mistakes have been discovered in a program, it should be _____ so it will work correctly.
5. A flowchart illustrates the logic of a program; it is a _____ representation of how the problem will be solved.
6. Program documentation should explain the program and make it easy to read and understand. Documentation is used _____ the way a program works.
7. Programs are _____ in the exact order in which the instructions are written; they are always carried out as the program specifies.
8. Computers cannot solve problems by themselves or think of any new ideas; computers, unlike people, cannot think _____.
9. A template, which contains the _____ of the geometrical shapes used in flowcharting, is used to draw neat diagrams.

Vocabulary Development

A. Answer the following questions based on the reading.

1. What are the geometrical names for the following symbols?

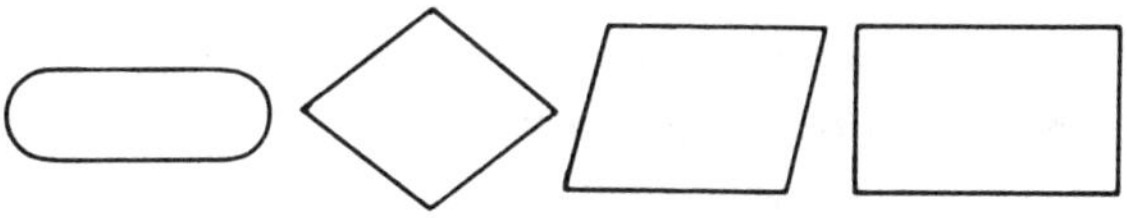

2. What do the following symbols mean?

   =   >=   >   <   <=

3. Match the symbol to its function in a flowchart.
   1. input/output 2. processing 3. start or end 4. decision

Comprehension Exercises

A. True-False. Write a "T" if the statement is true. Write "F" if it is false.

1. Computers can reason and think like human beings.
2. Programs should be carefully planned before they are written.
3. The program development cycle can help a programmer analyze a problem and write a program to solve the problem.

4. Testing is not a part of the program development cycle.
5. Flowcharting is the only method of representing the logic of a program.
6. A flowchart is a pictorial representation of the logic of a program.
7. Testing all the data must be done in order to find errors.
8. Documentation for programs should include explanations both within the program and outside of the program.
9. Geometrical symbols and mathematical symbols are used in flowcharts.
10. Flowcharting was developed by John von Neumann.

B. Choose the letter of the *best* answer for each of the following.

1. What is *not* true about computer programs?
   a. Programs must be written in a special way for the computer to be able to implement them.
   b. Programs carry out instructions exactly as they are written.
   c. Programs can be changed by the computer.
   d. Programs can be coded in different languages.

2. In the first stage of the program development cycle ____.
   a. the programmer analyzes all aspects of the problem
   b. the programmer designs the program
   c. the programmer begins to test the program
   d. the programmer analyzes the hardware requirements only

3. Which is *not* a step in the program development cycle?
   a. documenting the program
   b. inputting the program
   c. buying new hardware
   d. testing the program

4. Which represents the steps in the program development cycle in the correct order?
   a. testing, documenting, analyzing, coding, designing
   b. analyzing, designing, coding, testing, documenting
   c. analyzing, designing, testing, coding, documenting
   d. coding, analyzing, testing, documenting, designing

5. Which is *not* true of flowcharting?
   a. Flowcharts provide a means of communication between programmers.
   b. The logic of flowcharts should go from left to right.
   c. The notes inside the flowchart symbols are used for explanation.
   d. Templates must be used to draw flowcharts.

6. Flowcharts ____.
   a. are illustrations in program manuals
   b. are representations of the problems of individual programmers
   c. are pictorial representations of program decisions
   d. are pictorial representations of program logic
7. What illustrates the direction and order of the procedures in flowcharts?
   a. templates
   b. rectangles
   c. flowlines
   d. diamonds

Skill Enhancement

Modals

Modal auxiliaries are words which are combined with a verb to express mood. Modals can be used to express a change in mood in a present or past time.

A. The form for a non-past modal verb phrase is: modal auxiliary + base form of the verb.

Example: A programmer should plan the logic of a program before he writes it.

B. The negative form for a non-past modal verb phrase is: *modal auxiliary* + *not* + base form of the verb. The modals, except for *may*, may also be contracted.

Example: A programmer should not (shouldn't) write a program without planning it first.

C. Three of the modals have past forms, but do not necessarily refer to past time:

can–could   will–would   may–might

Example: Flowcharting is one method of program design that may be used.
Flowcharting is one method of program design that might be used.

The past of many modals is formed by using the modal perfect verb phrase: modal + *have* + past participle. This indicates that the action could have taken place, but did not.

Example: A program with many mistakes should have been reviewed before it was tested.

D. The negative of the modals have the following form: modal + *not* + base form of the verb. The negative modal form may also be contracted.

Example: A programmer should not (shouldn't) write a program without planning it first.

E. The modal auxiliaries that express necessity—*have to* and *must*—have the same meaning. The negatives of must and have to—*must not* and *do not have to*— do not have the same meaning. *Must not* means something is prohibited; *do not have to* means something is not necessary.

Example: A program must not be used before it is tested.
A program does not have to use all the data when it is tested.

F. The following summarizes the most common usage of the modal auxiliaries:

Ability:	can	Ability in past:	could
Possibility:	can	Possibility in past:	could
Impossibility:	could not		
Probability (slight):	may	might	could
Strong probability:	must		
Permission:	can	may (formal usage)	
Necessity:	must	have to	
Lack of necessity:	do not have to		
Prohibition:	must not	may not	can't
Recommendation (strong):	must		
Advisability:	should	ought to	
Future action:	will		

Skill Enhancement

A. Fill in the blanks with the correct form of the modal auxiliary. Refer to the reading if necessary. The first question has been done for you.

The third step in the program development cycle is coding the program. This is the actual writing of the program in a form the computer <u>can</u> (may/can) understand. Proper and accurate coding is very important and ____ (may/must) be done so that a program ____ (can/should) be easily understood or modified. Any computer language, like the ones discussed previously in this book, ____ (ought to/can) be used for coding the program. However, it is